THE
Negro's & Indians
ADVOCATE,
Suing for their Admiſſion into the
CHURCH
OR
A PERSUASIVE to the Inſtructing
and Baptizing of the *Negro's* and
Indians in our Plantations.

SHEWING,

That as the Compliance therewith can prejudice
no Mans juſt Intereſt; So the wilful Neglecting
and Oppoſing of it, is no leſs than a manifeſt
Apoſtacy from the Chriſtian Faith.

To which is added, A brief Account of Religion in *Virginia.*

By MORGAN GODWYN,
Sometime St. of Ch. Ch. Oxon.

Judges 19. 30. *And it was ſo, that all that ſaw it ſaid, There was
no ſuch deed done nor ſeen from the day that the Children of* Iſrael
came up out of the Land of Egypt, *unto this Day.*
Acts 4. 20. *We cannot but ſpeak the things which we have ſeen and heard.*

---

*If we muſt anſwer for our idle Words, how much more for our idle
ſilence?* St. Auguſtin.

LONDON, Printed for the Author, by *J. D.* and are
to be Sold by moſt Bookſellers. 1680.

Printing Statement:

Due to the very old age and scarcity of this book, many of the pages may be hard to read due to the blurring of the original text, possible missing pages, missing text and other issues beyond our control.

Because this is such an important and rare work, we believe it is best to reproduce this book regardless of its original condition.

Thank you for your understanding.

To the moſt Reverend Father in God, WILLIAM by Divine Providence, Lord Arch-Biſhop of *Canterbury*, his Grace; Of all *England* Primate and Metropolitan, and one of his Sacred Majeſties moſt Honourable Privy Council.

May it pleaſe your Grace,

IT *is at once both the Duty and Intereſt of theſe Papers to beſeech your Favour and Patronage, and to beg leave to carry in their Front a Name ſo ſacred; as being not only a Sanctuary from danger, and a Preſervative a-gainſt the infection and poyſon of Malicious Cen-ſures; but alſo ſo rich an Ornament, as in it ſelf ſuf-ficient to give them that Reputation and Luſtre which of themſelves they wanted, and to ſupply all the Defects and Errors of the unskilful Author.*

An Ambition I ſhould confeſs unpardonable, were the Temptation leſs, or the Subject meaner; which

A 3

in truth doth so much pertain to your Graces In-spection, that to have addressed themselves to any other, had been an alienation of your Graces Pro-perty, and no less than Sacrilege. Which being considered, I trust the apprehended Guilt will va-nish; And by that Acceptance, which your Graces wonted Humanity promises, the Crime will borrow another Name, and be transmuted into a Vertue.

I do not crave your Graces acceptance of these Papers upon any score of their Merit, unto which they dare not pretend; But do only beseech that charitable Kindness to be extended to them, which is due to Strangers: Especially coming so far, and upon such an Errand, as to implore Re-lief for those Myriads of hungry and distressed Souls abroad; most of them within the English Dominion, tho without their Care; and even vast Numbers being no other than our Peoples Slaves and Vassals; but from whom also the Bread of Life is most sacrilegiously detained. And by this your Condescention and Kindness to these stran-ger-Suppliants, it is not impossible, but that Bles-sing may be repeated to you, Of entertaining An-gels. The dignity of their Message being suffici-ent to qualifie them for those Titles and Names, which otherwise they durst not assume, and could no way challenge.

It would be but gross Impertinence for me to undertake to acquaint your Grace how zealous our

A1.

Ancestors were in promoting Works of this nature, the advancement of Religion in foraign Regions, even beyond their own Power, and Jurisdiction. Nor need I to mention how some others do make this very thing an Essential Mark of the Catholic Church, and from thence would prove their Religion true, and ours, at the same time, false: And do therefore conclude that they have sufficient grounds to unchurch us, and to determine us no Christian Nation. Nor shall I go about to parallel our Crime with that of the Ancient Britains, it being indeed much blacker; of whom yet Gildas complains (as a most grievous Impiety), that they never took care to preach the Gospel to the English and Saxons, their (not Domestics and Vassals, which these, we speak of, are, but) most cruel Invaders and Oppressors; and even to this he ascribes his Peoples and Countries overthrow. But instead thereof shall offer up my Prayers at the Throne of Mercy, that the like fatal, (but infinitely less excusable,) Neglect of our People abroad, not to say at Home also, may not prove alike Ominous, nor hasten the accomplishment of those Evils, which have so lately threatned, and do still hang over us; and of which, 'tis possible, that very mischievous and scandalous Neglect has been the prime occasion. And at the same time bemoan our hard Lot to be born and live in an Age so utterly barren of those Rich Fruits, with which the former did so abound: And that when

the

the most oppofite Parties *do compafs Sea and Land to make* Profelytes, *We only are charged with the* Neglect, *I fhall not add the oppofing of it; that being the* Crime *of fuch degenerated* Englifh, *who with that air, have imbibed the* Barbarity *and* Heathenifm *of the* Countries *they live in:* And *with whom, through the want of* Difcipline, Chrifti-anity *doth feem to be wholly loft, and nothing but* Infidelity *to have come in its place.*

And thus, I have given your Grace *the Motives inviting me to this bold attempt, together with thofe other for this* Publication; *which affuredly will not prove ineffectual whilft your* Grace *fhall continue what you have always been:* It *being impoffible that that flame of* Religious Zeal, *which hath hitherto fo vigoroufly acted in your* Grace, *fhould be* Extinguifhed *whilft you are alive; But muft needs excite you to further endeavours for the good of* Souls, *tho at a remoter diftance than both the* India's; *or that you fhould fuffer a thing of that* Confequence *for to fleep.* Which *doubt-lefs will give you a* Name *in the bleffed Records of* Eternity, *equal to thofe* Primitive Pious Bifhops *and holy* Patriarchs, *who have been moft* Induftrious *and* Vigilant *in publifhing the* Doctrine, *and promoting the* Service *of their* Lord *and* Saviour.

But I begin to be tedious, nor will your Graces *occafions of greateft* Moment, *admit of*

unneceffary Avocations : Wherefore (to avoid
being further troublesome) I fhall humbly fub-
mit this whole Affair to your Graces Wifdom
and Conduct, and no lefs my felf to your difpo-
fal : As being

My Lord,

Your Graces moft Dutiful

and Obedient Servant, and

moft Devoted Orator,

M. Godwyn.

The

( )

THE

PREFACE.

THe ſtate of Religon in the Plantations is ſuch, as that to ſtir up all Mens Zeal and Commiſeration, there needs no other Argument than its being rightly underſtood and known.

This is induſtriouſly avoided and prevented by ſuch, who as public Agents for thoſe parts, ſhould in the firſt place repreſent the Wants and Grievances thereof ; being of greateſt conſequence both to The Souls of Men, and to the Government under which they live, and by which they are Protected and Imployed ; and therefore ought in Conſcience to preſerve it.

But the Goſpel being become ſtale News, and thoſe glad Tidings ſounding but as ſome Anile Fable or Dream, the neceſſity of this needleſs and troubleſome Charge about Religion, cannot enter into ſuch, who for the moſt part do know no other God but Money, nor Religion but Profit. Which, with ſome other prouder Conſiderations, provokes them to obſtruct all deſigns for the good of thoſe Churches, and to report all things already ſo well ſettled, as not needing the leaſt amendment or alteration. Preſu-
ming

ming (belike) that no half-starved Caitiff coming from those parts, will be so hardy as to gain-say Men in Authority, befriended with the Purses and Power of whole Provinces to defend them; and thereby enabled to support their own, and to blast any other the most innocent Man's Reputation.

But being my self fully perswaded, that God will assuredly make good his Promise to the World, of causing his Gospel to be published, his Name called upon, and his Church established among the remotest Nations, I have here attempted to break through this Opposition; and as not knowing how to justifie my silence, which perchance might be more safe; without any regard to those Gentlemens displeasure, which I must expect even to the utmost degree; I do here tender to the Public this Plea both for the Christianizing of our Negro's and other Heathen in those Plantations, and for settling (or rather reviving) of Religion amongst our own People there.

And as the Epidamnians (a Colony also, but oppressed by a Faction) coming to Corcyra their Mother-Country, are said to have pointed to their Ancestors Sepulchres, and chalenging Kindred with them, did thence infer their natural Right to relief and assistance from those Corcyreans; So I doubt not but, besides these, (which are no less true, and may as well be alledged by us,) many nobler Considerations will prevail for the Relief of those parts. For our Church being, as is too evident, indebted to the Wise and Unwise, to the Barbarians and others, both Bond and Free; how can she, the former Veil being removed, forbear to impart her Bread, the Word of Eternal Life, to the many wretched Souls there, who do daily perish through the want thereof?

Thucyd. l. 1.

Rather

Rather as St. Paul's Macedonian, Acts 16. *suing for help, was to him an infallible token, that God had called him to preach the Gospel unto them;* so I question not but the miserable state of those People thus represented to our most Reverend Fathers and Country-Men, and alike needing and imploring their help, may stir up the same Zeal and pious Sentiments; and in the end prove no less effectual for the propagating and preserving of Christianity in those Colonies. And since the detecting of Conspiracies against Religion, *is a work so grateful, as at this time doth especially appear;* I hope I shall deserve no blame (from good People) for thus offering my Mite of Discovery also; not against some one Party or Division in Religion, *but of a more dangerous Conspiracy, even against* Christianity it self, with the very Life and Being thereof. To defend and preserve which, against the Hellish contrivances of our Anti-Religionists (*such as we find,* Acts 13. 8. *and who are grown very numerous,*) ought to be the united and joynt endeavours of all Persons (of what Sect or Party soever) who do retain any Sense or Affection for it : *Each Soul vowing with himself,* (in the Comedians *Language*) Nunquam eam se deserturum, non si capiundos sciat esse inimicos omnes Homines : And resolving not to desist from prosecuting those Enemies to God and Man (its implacable Adversaries,) until they are exterminated from off the face of the Earth. We having certainly as much reason to be zealous for Christ's Laws, as those Heathens, who thought a bare Inscription on their Graves, a sufficient reward and recompence for bravely attempting (tho perishing in) the defence of their Countries.

Dic Hospes Spartanos te hic
vidisse jacentes,
Dum Sanctis Patriæ legibus
obsequimur.

But here 'tis possible that they may be apt (as 'tis certain they have Confidence enough) to deny this whole
Charge,

Charge, even to their refusal of the Christianizing of their Slaves, were it a thing less known. But this last being so manifestly true, can any Man once so much as doubt of the rest? There being (questionless) nothing so black, which he for his profit (if with impunitie) will not perpetrate, who, without scruple, can so glibly swallow that Impiety. Nor is it against Charity to think the worst of one, who, by that single Omission, lives in a perpetual contempt of Christianity, and hourly affronts that Faith he professeth to believe. And I do here once for all declare, That whatever Passages I have in this Discourse delivered of them, are either what have proceeded from my own Knowledg, as being an Eye or Ear Witness, and (perhaps) a Patient under them; or else which have been attested to me by Persons of as great Veracity and Credit, as any those parts do afford, (of whom divers are now residing in England); who could have no design in the Imposture, and therefore are not by me in the least suspected. Nay further, even themselves, (unless resolved to be Perjur'd upon Record, if examined upon Oath, must confess as much. Nor do I desire any thing more, than to be brought upon a Justification; which they cannot but know can never (here) succeed to their Advantage. And for their Threats (I have heard) of throwing Dirt, and smiting with their Tongues, (besides that this is but a shifting off of the Question); as they shall not take me unprepared, so let them know, that whilst I have this shelter to flie unto,

Nil conscire mihi, nullâ & pallescere culpâ;

the very worst they can vomit forth will never in the least prejudice me in the opinion and esteem of Good Men.

Lastly, Whereas some may perchance object against my spending Time in this Discourse to prove the Negro's
Hu-

Humanity, *and to shew that neither their* Complexion *nor* Bondage, Descent *nor* Country, *can be any impediment thereto.* Tho I have spoken to it, Pag. 13. *and else-where, yet here I shall further give this Answer, That this is as needful (the contrary being believed, or at least made a pretence) as any of the rest. And here let the Objecters also remember, that a thousand Years since, it had been as ridiculous for any Man to go about to prove that* Bread *was* Bread, *and not* Flesh: *Whereas now the greatest Divines of both the* Protestant *and* Romish *Persuasion, have thought it no disparagement to their Learning, to write large Volumns, the one for, but the other against that Faith. And for other (whether Imaginary or Real) defects in this Discourse, if Charity and the goodness of the Design will not veil them, I hope that at least it may find some mitigation of the Censure, from the consideration of its being written in* Terra barbara.

The

The CONTENTS.

The INTRODUCTION.

WHerein the Temper and Inclination of our People in Barbados, &c. as to the promoting of Chriſtianity among their Slaves, &c. is deſcribed; and the Motives for writing this Diſcourſe are ſhewed, with the Neceſſity thereof. Page 1.

Errata.

PAge 24. read *Herm-aphrodite*. P. 31. r. Καν. P. 38. r. *ἰερα*, for *modo*. P. 44. l. 12. r: *could*. P. 48. l. 26. r. 2. 5, 6. f. 7. 8. P. 52. l. 26. f. [. *The*, r. *the*] & dele *doth*. and l. 31. before *and, make*). P. 63, 64. r. *δελεια* and *δελιω*. P. 113. (otherwise 97) l. 23. f. *here*, r. *so*. P. 114. (or 98) l. 16. r. *persuade*. P. 116 (or 100) l. 28. r. *emptie*. P. 119 (or 103) l. 13. r. *in*, f. *of*. P. 128. l. 17. r. *who*, f. *and*. P. 171. l. 4. and 11. r. *him*, f. *them*. l. 10. r. *his*, f. *their*.

THE
NEGRO'S and INDIANS
ADVOCATE,
SUING
For their Admiſſion into the Church.
OR,
A PERSUASIVE to the Inſtructing and Baptizing the *Negro's* and *Indians* in our
PLANTATIONS.

Shewing that as the complying therewith can be no
Prejudice to any Man's juſt Intereſt ; ſo the wilful
Neglecting and Oppoſing of it, is no leſs than a ma-
nifeſt Apoſtacy from the Chriſtian Faith.

The INTRODUCTION.

*Wherein the Temper and Inclination of our People here
(viz. in* Barbados *) as to the Promoting of Chriſtianity among their Slaves, or other Heathen, is Deſcribed ;
and the Motives for writing this Diſcourſe are ſhewed,
with the Neceſſity thereof.*

§. I. IT having been *my Lot* ſince my Arrival upon
this Iſland, to fall ſometimes into Diſcourſes
touching the neceſſity of *Inſtructing* our
Negro's and other *Heathen* in the *Chriſtian Faith,* and of *Baptizing* them (both which I
obſerved were generally neglected ;) I ſeldom

B   or

of never miffed of oppofition from fome one of thefe three forts of People: The firft, Such, as by reafon of the Difficulty and Trouble, affirmed it not only Impracticable, but alfo Impoffible. The fecond, Such who lookt upon all Defigns of that Nature, as too much favouring *of Popifh Supererrogation*, and not in the leaft Expedient or Neceffary. The third, Such (and thefe I found the moft numerous) who abfolutely condemned both the Permiffion and Practice thereof, as deftructive to their Intereft, tending to no lefs Mifchief than the overthrow of their Eftates, and the ruine of their *Lives*, threatning even the utter *Subverfion* of the Ifland. Who therefore have always been very watchful to fecure that Door, and wifely to prevent all *fuch mifchievous Enterprizes*. Themfelves in the mean time imploying their utmoft Skill and Activity *to render the Defign Ridiculous*; thereby to affright the better difpofed (if any) from ever confenting to an Act, which, beyond all peradventure, would fo much call their *Difcretion and Wifdom* into Queftion.

2. This fpirit of *Gentilifm* (for that is the mildeft Name it will deferve) was principally occafioned through the want of care in the feating of thefe *Colonies*, where *Religion* ought to have been planted together with the firft Inhabitants; as amongft *all Chriftians, befides our felves*, hath elfewhere been generally practifed: But the *Englifh*, for being of the *beft Religion*, are to be excufed. 'Tis true, the *Negro's* ignorance of our Language was for fome time a real *Impediment* thereto, and fo long a tolerable plea for the *Omiffion*; but none afterward, when they had arrived to an ability of Underftanding, and difcourfing in *Englifh* equal with moft of our *own People*; which *many thoufands* of them long fince have: Whilft now after fuch a long Risk of *Licentioufnefs*, an *ungodly Cuftom*

ftom grown ftrong, is kept as a Law: To gain-fay which is lookt upon as no lefs *impious*, than elfewhere it is (and formerly it univerfally was) *reputed Meritorious*.

3. Now to reprefent this more plaufible to the World, another no lefs difingenuous and unmanly *Pofition* hath been formed; and privately *(and as it were in the dark)* handed to and again, which is this, That the *Negro's*, though in their Figure they carty fome refemblances of Manhood, yet are indeed *no Men.* A Conceit like unto which I have read, was fome time fince invented by the *Spaniards*, to juftifie *their murthering the Americans.* But for this here, I may fay, that if *Atheifm and Irreligion* were the true Parents who gave it Life, furely *Sloth and Avarice* have been no unhandy Inftruments and Affiftants to midwife it into the World, and to Fofter and Nurfe it up. Under whofe Protection getting abroad, it hath acquired fufficient ftrength and reputation to fupport it felf; being now able not only to maintain its ground, but to bid defiance to all its *Oppofers*; who in truth are found to be but very *few*, and thofe fcarcely *confiderable.* The iffue whereof is, That as in the *Negroe's all pretence to Religion* is cut off, fo their *Owners* are hereby fet at Liberty, and freed from thofe importunate Scruples, which Confcience and better Advice might at any time happen to inject into their unfteadie Minds. A *Fiction* hardly to be parallel'd throughout the Fables of the *Poets*; and which I prefume never before found entertainment amongft any, befide thofe above mentioned; or perhaps our *Neighbours of* Holland, *whofe Religion is alfo governed by their Trade*, and (as hath, I fear, been *too juftly charged* upon them) for the fake thereof fhall be *denied.*

4. Now whilft in my thoughts I reflected upon thefe wild *Fancies* and abfurd *Pofitions*, which I had often heard (tho not in exprefs words, yet in *terms*

æqui-

equivalent) no lefs impudently urged and afferted, than I faw *univerfally practifed.* A petty *Reformado* Pamphlet was put into my hand by an *officious* FRIEND, or *Quaker* of this Ifland, (I fuppofe, in order to my *Converfion*); upon the perufal whereof, which was ftrictly enjoyned me, I met with this malitious (but crafty) *Invective*, levelled againft the *Minifters*, to whom it was by the way of *Interrogatory*, directed and applied in no other than thefe words : " *Who* " *made you Minifters of the Gofpel to the White People only,* " *and not to the Tawneys and Blacks alfo?* (with many other the like infolent *Queries*, following in a *tedious Harangue*, I think, to this effect, for I fhall not undertake to rehearfe his words exactly): " Why do you " not teach your People in this part of their Duty, or " at leaft fhew them the way by *your Example, begin-* " *ning at HOME with thofe of your OWN FAMI-* " *LIES*, whom you cannot deny but you neglect as " much as you do the reft? What fhould be the Rea- " fon that you fpend fo much time in Railing againft " us, whom you call *Quakers*, and other peaceable " People ; but where there *is Occafion*, have not a word " to fay? As if this Ignorance of Chrift in them were " not as well worth your Pains and falfe Zeal, as the " beating down of Phanaticifm, as you are pleafed to " term Innocent People's belief and perfuafions? Doth " not *this filence* proceed from a *fear of Men*, whom " you are loth to difpleafe by this Doctrine, for what " covetous ends your felves beft know? And do you " not thereby teftifie that you are *Men-pleafers* and " *Hirelings*; but not the *Servants of God*, nor as you " falfely pretend *Minifters of Jefus Chrift*, who, as " your *Catechifm* (if you ever read it) doth con- " fefs, came to *Redeem all Mankind*, without excep- " ting NEGRO'S *and* INDIANS? And therefore " his *Minifters* and *Apoftles* were by him commanded

" to

" *to preach the Gospel to all the World,* and *to be Witnesses*
" *of him to the uttermost parts of the Earth.* Is this the
" way to set forward the Salvation of *all Men* ; and to
" make the Ways of God and of the *Gospel* known
" unto *all Nations, and to all Conditions* of Men there-
" in, not omitting *Slaves,* nor any other ? Is this to pre-
" pare the Way of Jesus Christ against his second com-
" ing to judge the World, *by turning the Hearts of the*
" *Disobedient to the wisdom of the Just,* and to approve
" your selves faithful and true Pastours, earnestly feeding
" the Flock of Christ, and preaching his Word unto
" them, as in your *Collects* (as you call them) you pre-
" tend to pray ? Is this to follow the Saints in all
" Godly and Vertuous Living, who as you reade, *Mark*
" *the 16th and the last Verse, went forth preaching every*
" *where,* and ventured their Lives into all the World
" to preach the Gospel to the Heathen, when you neg-
" lect it in your *Parishes and Families ?* Is this to take
" upon you the Office of a Minister, to serve God for
" the promoting of his Glory, and the edifying of his
" People committed to your care and charge ? Is this
" to be ready with all faithful diligence to use both
" publick and private Monitions and Exhortations,
" as well to the Sick, as to the whole within your
" Cures ? Is this to be diligent to frame and fashion
" your own *Lives and your Families* according to the
" Doctrine of Christ, and to make both your selves
" and them, as much as in you lieth, wholesome *Ex-*
" *amples and Patterns* to the Flock of Christ, laying
" aside all study of the *World* and the *Flesh ?* For
" shame cease to call your selves *Christ's Ministers,* un-
" less you will be contented to work in Christ's *Vine-*
" *yard,* to preach his Doctrine truly, and to exhort
" and edifie *the poor of his Flock,* as he commanded
" you ; and to testifie both to small and great, *bond*
" *and free,* (as his Apostles and Ministers did) *the*
B 3 " *whole*

"*whole Counsel of God*, left hereafter you be found *par-*
"*tial in your selves*, against which both *Paul* and
"*James* do warn you, &c. This was the scope and
substance of our *Quakers Harangue* (if my Memory fails
me not) with a great deal more to the same purpose,
which I have neither *will* nor *leasure* here to repeat;
what I have already delivered, being sufficient to silence us as to any *Reply*, besides that of the Poet,

———— *Pudet hæc opprobria nobis*
Et dici potuisse, & non potuisse refelli.

The *Duties* there by him urged, (tho doubtless with
curst intent, and as *Judas* became Spokesman and Orator *for the Poor*) being evident from the avowed *Prin-*
ciples of all Christians; no less then from *the express*
words of our own Liturgie, by him collected from the
several parts thereof : As will be seen upon the peru-
sal of the Collect for the *Ember Weeks*, the general
Prayer *for all conditions of Men*, the Collect for *Good*
Friday, that for the *second Sunday in Advent*, and for
St.*Peter's*, and *All-Saints Days*; and lastly, from the *Re-*
sponses in the Book of *Ordination of Priests and Deacons.*
And the *Neglect* reprehended, being too apparent to
be either shifted off, or *extenuated* by any palliation,
or excuse.

5. Now upon this I began to question with my self,
If the Gospel be *good Tidings*, why should it be con-
cealed, or hid ? And since designed so *to all People*,
why should not these partake of it as well as others ?
If we are bound to *pray* for their Conversion, why
are we not also to *endeavour* it ? And since that our
Blessed Lord commanded his Apostles, St. *Mat.* 28. *to*
go and make Disciples of ALL the Heathen, why may it
not be alike lawful for me, with the great Apostle, *Heb.*
2. 8. to both argue and conclude. *In that he said All,*

be

be had excepted none ? I then also fell to reflect upon the Doom of the *unprofitable Servant* ; and that since Christ had been thus merciful to me, *putting me into the Ministry,* so unworthy of it ; I could have no pretence to be silent ; and that I ought not *to lay my* (tho slender) *Talent up in a Napkin,* lest thereby I should justly incur the like sad Doom. And withal, observing that no abler *Advocate* for them had appeared, I concluded my self under some Obligation, to endeavour to wipe off these Blemishes, and to repair the Honour of our *Religion and Profession.* But withal, chiefly to admonish our People of this Neglect ; and if *possible,* to convince them of the wickedness of those horrid *Positions* and *Principles* before mentioned ; as also of the necessity of their *speedy applying* themselves to that great Duty hitherto so *unchristianly omitted.* Whereupon my thoughts after some time, resolved themselves into these three general *Assertions.*

1. That the Negro's (*both Slaves and others*) have naturally an equal Right *with other Men to the* Exercise and Privileges *of* Religion ; *of which 'tis most unjust in any part to deprive them.*

2. That the profession of Christianity *absolutely obliging to the promoting of it,* no Difficulties nor *Inconveniences, how great soever, can excuse* the Neglect, *much less* the hindering *or opposing of it, which is in effect no better than a renunciation of that Profession.*

3. That the Inconveniencies here pretended *for this Neglect,* being examined, *will be found nothing such, but rather the contrary.*

And this I do the more confidently here undertake from the encouragement and counsel of the *Wise Man,* Eccles. 11. 6. thus advising: *In the morning*

sow

sow thy seed, and in the evening withhold not thine Hand, for thou knowest not whether shall prosper, either this or that, or whether they both shall prove alike good. And as not in the least despairing of a due success, tho even *Briars and Thorns should be with me, and my dwelling should be among Scorpions;* since the Almighty hath by the Mouth of his Evangelical Prophet given us this assurance, *Isa.* 55. *That as the Rain cometh down, and the Snow from Heaven, and returneth not thither, but watereth the Earth, and maketh it bring forth and bud, that it may give Seed to the sower, and Bread to the eater: So shall my Word be, that goeth forth out of my Mouth; it shall not return unto me void, but it shall accomplish that which I please, and it shall prosper in the thing whereunto I sent it.*

Ezek. 8. 9.

And he said unto me, Go in, and behold the wicked Abominations that they do here.

CHAP

CHAP. I.

That the Negro's (both Slaves and others) have naturally an equal Right with other Men, to the Exercise and Privileges of Religion ; of which 'tis most unjust in any part to deprive them.

§. I. ANd thus our *Negro's* and *Indian's* case as to Religion being sum'd up and truly stated, and our People's temper and inclination towards the Conversion of them being represented ; I betake my self to my first general Assertion ; which I shall divide into these three *Propositions.*

1. *First,* That *naturally* there is in every Man an equal *Right to Religion.*
2. *Secondly,* That *Negro's* are Men, and therefore are invested with the *same Right.*
3. *Thirdly,* That being thus qualified and invested, to deprive them of this *Right* is the *highest injustice.*

1. For the first of these, *viz. That naturally there is in every Man such a Right :* There are none can easily doubt, who do understand either *what Religion is,* or the true end *for which Man was made ;* namely, *to glorifie and serve God ;* which is no other than to be *Religious.* Now this being the certain *End* for which Man was made, a *Right* to perform that *End* cannot be denied him.

2. Which *Right* was not superinduced as an additional supply of any imaginary defects of his Creation, but was at first planted and formed in him. Nor doth he injoy it in common with other *Animals,* but

claims

claims it as his special Privilege peculiar to him [*as Man*], and in a distinct manner from the rest of the Creation : Nothing here besides being indued with a Capacity suitable, and therefore not *pretending* thereunto.

3. And as Man alone lays claim to this high *Privilege*, so it is most certainly *every Man's*, there being none so despicable or base, but hath as unquestionable a *Right* thereto, as the most illustrious and wise Virtuoso; holding the same equally and *in common* with all others of the like *species* with himself. The reason whereof is, because he claims it upon the account of his being Man, and only [*as such*] hath that Right. Now, *Quatenus & de omni reciprocantur* : As also, *A quatenus ad omne valet consequentia,* say the Logicians: That is, whatsoever is avouchable of any Creature [*as such*], must be equally true of every individual Branch and Member of the *whole kind or species* ; all being equal sharers in those *common* gifts of *Nature*.

4. As for Instance : The *sensitive Faculties*, as Seeing, Hearing, Smelling, *&c.* As also the natural *appetite* to Food, desire of Sleep and Rest, with other the like *affections*, are common to all *Animals* ; but not to *Plants* or *Vegetables*, because *peculiar* only to the other. These they do claim [*as such*], and therefore may not be denied to any the most inconsiderable *Animal* of the whole Creation. For, being thereof once deprived, they instantly cease to be, or to be reputed [*such*.]

5. Even so, *Ex tot generibus nullum est Animal,* &c. said the *Roman Orator* ; Of all Creatures here below, Man only hath the notion of a *Deity*, and a propriety in *Religion*. Which *Right and Propriety* doth belong unto him only upon the account of his being Man ; that is, because he is endued with a reasonable and immortal Soul, which alone constitutes him *a Man*,
and

and capacitates him for *Religion.* For without this he were not *a Man*; could neither be *fubject* to Laws or *Difcipline*, nor capable of *Rewards* or Punifhments after this Life : Nor in a word, could be any longer feparated, *à grege brutorum*, as the Poet fpeaks: Above whom he is only advanced by that Prerogative of *Reafon* implanted in his Soul, the only proper and apt feat for *Religion.*

6. For that the Soul of Man is that alone, which qualifies and enables him to be *Religious*, and that Man's groffer and heavier parts do contribute nothing thereunto, is manifeft : For that *Religion* being an exercife wherein the Mind and Underftanding only are concerned, the Body abftracted from thefe, (by whom it is to be led and directed) can fupply no other part in this Work, than of a fecondary Agent therein, and as *fubfervient* to the other. For otherwife *Atheifts*, and refolved wicked Men, *might ferve God* and be Religious; whilft like *Engines* compelled thereto, their Bodies fhewed fome little compliance with the prefent Action, fo far as *outward Geftures* would go; tho they believed nothing of the work they were about : and even a Beaft might be taught to do the like; but could never be governed *by Laws*, be reduced under *Difcipline* and *Government* (of which Man by his underftanding is alone capable) or be fubject to the *impreffions of Confcience*; have a profpect of Happinefs, or be apprehenfive of future Dangers and Contingencies; much lefs be able to provide againft them. All thefe Faculties being peculiar to the *Rational Being*, or Soul, feated in Man only : Of whofe *Species*, if our *Negro's* can be truly faid to partake, then will it of neceffity follow, that they are *Originally* ftated in the like *Natural Right* to the Privileges of *Religion.* The thing that I am next to prove.

§. II.

§. II. 1. I muſt confeſs the *Antecedent* is by our *Anti Religioniſts*, (as was at firſt remembred) and even by ſome others who would be thought leſs Enemies *to Piety*, with no ſmall reſolution oppoſed, tho not always expreſsly, yet in words equivalent, and withal moſt fully explained by their ſubſequent daily Practice. Which Practice, becauſe their words may be capable of a milder conſtruction, (tho in this caſe not in the leaſt deſerving it); I intend for the ſole, at leaſt chief Rule or Meaſure to judge of and to underſtand the other. And here let no one account it incredible, that *Intereſt* ſhould ſeduce Men into ſuch a *monſtrous opinion*, (which divers even in *England* have been heard to defend) and (as prejudging the cauſe and matter) conclude it time miſpent, in labouring to refute it : But remember how much *ſtranger opinions*, a much greater part of the World upon the like Motive have elſewhere, *tho in another kind*, embraced. And as to this, there wanting not *Irrational* Creatures, ſuch as the Ape and Drill, that do carry with them ſome reſemblances of Men. The too frequent unnatural conjunctions (as *Taverneir* diſcourſeth in his Voyages) of ſome *Africans* with thoſe Creatures, (tho not ſo as to Unpeople that great Continent) giving occaſion for ſuch ſurmiſes as to ſome few *there*, tho never of any that were brought *hither* ; our *Factors* being too worldly wiſe to commit ſuch groſs overſights in their *Civil* Affairs, whatever greater may eſcape them in their *Spiritual*. And the *Spaniards* queſtion (which the ſame *Taverneir* alſo mentions) touching the Brutality of the *Americans*, (and, which I have heard was held in the *Affirmative* in one of the *Univerſities of Spain*) ſerving not a little to make my report more credible ; and to acquit me of all *fictitious Romancing* herein. Wherefore it being granted for poſſible that

ſuch

such wild Opinions, by the inducement and instiga-
tion of our Planters chief
Deity, *Profit*, may have lodged themselves in the Brains
of some of us; I shall not
fear to betake my self to the
refuting of this one which
I have spoken of. For the
effecting of which, me-
thinks, the consideration of
the shape and figure of our
Negro's Bodies, their Limbs
and Members; their Voice
and Countenance, in all
things according with other
Mens; together with their

*Since my return to Eng-
land, the Reverend D of
H. told me, that an Inha-
bitant of B. being by himself
urged to get his attendant
Negro's Baptized, made
the like Objections, with
those which he found re-
cited in the Papers I shewed him, which were no other
than a part of this Book.
And tho such Practices may
seem strange to People in
England, yet the same Persons going thither are sud-
denly changed, so that they
make nothing of it.*

Rifibility and *Discourse* (Man's *peculiar* Faculties)
should be a sufficient Conviction. How should they
otherwise be capable of *Trades*, and other no less Man-
ly imployments; as also of *Reading and Writing*; or
shew so much Discretion in management of *Business*;
eminent in divers of them; but wherein (we know)
that many of our own People are *deficient*, were they
not truly Men? These being the most clear *emanations*
and results of *Reason*, and therefore the most genuine
and perfect characters of *Homoniety*, if I may so speak.
Or why should they be tormented and whipt almost
(and sometimes quite) to death, upon any, whether
small or great Miscarriages, it is not material, were they
(like Brutes) naturally destitute of *Capacities* equal to
such undertakings? Or why should their *Owners*,
Men of Reason no doubt, conceive them fit to exercise the place of Governours and *Overseers* to their *fellow Slaves*, which is frequently done, if they were but
meer Brutes? Since nothing beneath the *Capacity* of
a Man might rationally be presumed proper for those

Duties and Functions, wherein so much of understanding, and a more than *ordinary* Apprehension is
required. It would certainly be a pretty kind of *Co-
mical* Frenzie, to imploy Cattel about Business, and
to constitute them *Lieutenants, Overseers,* and *Governours,* like as *Domitian* is said to have made his Horse
a *Consul.*

2. Their Objections against this, are poor and tri-
vial; yet because with a great many here, seeming to
carry no little weight, (for otherwise they could never both argue and act so absurdly, as they do); And
because found serviceable to their great *End,* which I
have before spoken of, not rejected by the Wiser; they
must not, *sily and idle as they be,* for these Reasons be
slighted. They are of divers sorts. The first whereof are certain impertinent and blasphemous *distortions
of Scripture*; out of which they would fain bribe
four places, to wit, in *Genesis* 1. 27, 28. and 2. 7.
and 4. 15. and lastly, 9. 25, 26. to give in *evidence*
for them. Now in the two first of these they strain
hard to derive our *Negro's* from a stock *different* from
Adam's: but by the third, they bespeak them as de-
scendents from *Cain,* and to carry his *Mark*: And yet
by the last, as if *condemned* to contradictions, they
make them the Posterity of that unhappy Son of *Noah,*
who, they say, was, together with his whole *Family*
and Race, *cursed* by his *Father.* Of which *Curse* 'tis
worth the observing what *blessed use* they to themselves
do make, and what variety of advantages they thereby reap. For from thence, as occasion shall offer,
they'll infer their *Negro's Brutality*; justifie their
reduction of them under Bondage; disable them from
all *Right and Claims,* even to *Religion* it self; pronounce them *Reprobates,* and upon a sudden (with
greater speed and cunning than either the nimblest
Jugler, or Witch.) *transmute* them into whatsoever
substance

fubftance the, *exigence* of their wild reafonings fhall drive them to.

3. I confefs, as for the third of thefe, which is *Cain's Mark*, they infift not much upon it, becaufe thwarting their *Pre-Adamitifm*, of which they are extreamly fond, tho many times 'tis by their lefs skilful Difputants *preft to the Service*. But the *Pre-Adamites* whimfey, which is preferred above the *Curfe* (becaufe fo exceeding ufeful to undermine the *Bible* and *Religion*, unto both which they have vowed never to be *reconciled*) they believe invincible; tho upon but a very fuperficial trial, found (as will inftantly appear) to be in fome things *falfe*, in other,*empty* and *filly*; but in nothing, of any confiderable *weight* or moment. For the fuller proof whereof, I fhall crave leave to refer the *Reader* to that no lefs *Learned* than *Judicious* Perfon, *Judge Hales*, in his Book lately publifhed concerning the *Origination of Man*, wherein the whole *Myftery* of that foul *Herefie* is unravelled, and moft ftrongly refuted.

4. But that I may not feem wholly to fhift my Reader off to that *Reverend* Author, and as it were fhelter my *floth and ignorance* (which laft doth, I confefs, ftand in need of fuch an able *Supporter*) under his learned Pen, I fhall beg his patience a little, whilft I take upon me to entertain him with fome two or three of that learned Doctor's *Arguments*, who was the firft *Author* of that Opinion; all by him borrowed from *Gen.* 4. 2. &c. from whence he undertakes to confirm his unheard of *Hypothefis*.

5. Of which, the firft I fhall attempt to unbowel is that, wherein he takes it for granted, (I cannot point out the *Chapter* and *Page*, it being long fince I read it) that before the *commencement* of that *Hiftory*, there muft be a numerous race of Men, not derivable from *Adam*. For firft he there obferves, that *Abel*

was a *Keeper* (the *Hebrew,* as our Margen alſo directs us, ſaith a *Feeder*) of *Sheep.* This without more ado he concludes was to *ſecure* them, not from ſtraying or being devoured by Wolves, but from being *ſtolen:* And by whom? Not by his *Parents,* or *Brother,* that being unlikely ; but by other Sheep-ſtealing *Rovers* of the pretended former *Creation.*

6. Secondly, he obſerves from the ſame Chapter, that *Cain was a Tiller of Ground,* that is, an Husbandman. This, ſaith he, doth ſuppoſe divers *Trades* to be at the ſame time in being ; to wit, *Smiths, Plow-Wrights, Carpenters,* &c. to furniſh him with Inſtruments of Husbandry. (The like he might have inferred, and 'twas a groſs overſight if he did not, from *Adam's* being put to dreſs *Eden; Gardening-Tools* (tho 'tis ſaid, *that there was not a Man to make them*) being as requiſite for that work, as *Plows* for the other). But had this learned Man travelled the more Southern parts of *A-frica;* or moſt, if not all the parts of *America;* he might perhaps there have learned a more *Orthodox Comment* upon theſe *Texts,* and more decently have ſolved his Doubts. For there he might have beheld the *Natives* (probably ſtill retaining the faſhion of thoſe *Elder* times) planting each Man his own provi-ſion of *Maiz;* room being firſt made for the Seed to paſs into the Ground with no ſubtiler *Engine* than a ſimple Stick thruſt into it, or it may be with his *Finger:* And after this weeding his Corn with *Fiſh ſhells,* in-ſtead of *Hoa's,* uſed by the *Engliſh,* and other wiſer People. And this they ſtill practiſe, without craving the leaſt aſſiſtance (unleſs, poſſibly, ſome few of them ſince our Arrival) from thoſe Trades; of which, as indeed of almoſt all other, they are wholly igno-rant.

7. Thirdly, turning to the *Septuagint* Bible, he there reades that *Cain,* talking with his Brother, invites him

in

in these words, Διέλθωμεν εἰς τὸ πεδίον, to go into the Field. From which Clause, not found in the *Hebrew*, he is sure they must needs at that time dwell in some *Town* or *City*, not so soon to be built by *Adam's* thin *Race*. And therefore other *Architects* and Workmen must be fetcht from that imaginary *Elder Creation* But this *Logic*, even admitting that Clause, would never hold in *Virginia*, where there is neither Town nor City (their *Metropolis* excepted, lately consisting of some twelve or fourteen Families, but since the late *Rebellion* and Burning of it, I suppose of fewer) throughout that, nor even the Neighbouring *Provinces*. And even in this *Island*, we know that Men do not always take their way thorow the *Bridg-Town* into their *Plantations*. And no more necessity was there for *Cain* and *Abel's* not doing the same. And here also the *Natives* (and I shall suppose no less of the South of *Africa*) could have taught him to erect places for Shelter and Lodging, such as 'tis possible both *Adam* and his *Children* for a long time might be contented with, without the aid of *Masons* or other *Builders*, than what were needful for platting of *Arbours*, covered only with *Leaves*, or the *Bark* of Trees, which generally are the *Royal Mansions* and *Basilicks* of their greatest Kings and Emperours. But this *Eutopian* or *Atlantean* City, having no Foundation nor being, any where extant, but in our *Quixots* rambling *Fancy*, there is no need to produce either Builders, or Inhabitants for it.

8. However, to put an end to this Dispute: There is no doubt but that these places in *Genesis*, viz. Chap. 2. 5. & 3. 20. & 7. 21, 22, 23. and 10. 32. All levelled as it were expresly against this Doctrine of *Pre-Adamitism*, (as the learned *Judge* hath observed) do certainly carry in them no less truth, than those other, which its first Author, (contrary to

C

the

the sense and judgment of the whole World, both *Jews* and *Christians*, who have gone before him) hath *wrested* to that his wicked purpose; and ought with as great certainty to be believed. So also doth Saint *Paul's* affirmation at *Athens*, in the hearing of the Wits and Virtuosi there, (who refused not to acquiesce with him in the same judgment) *That God had made* [*of one Blood*] *all Nations of Men, for to dwell on all the face of the Earth*, Acts 17. 26. I say, these with many other weighty Arguments and Testimonies from *sacred Scripture*, ought to challenge from us at least an equal measure of credit with those Dreams of that *Fantastic Author*: And may no less at the same time inform us, how misbecoming *Wise Men* and *Christians* it is (without consideration of what may be said on either side) in a moment to run down and explode such *ancient received Principles*, for an irrational *Novelty*, never before thought on; and thus to shake the foundation of the Christian Faith, only to gratifie a *silly Humour*, and to shew *how bold they dare be with the Almighty*. Who yet, if they are resolved not to be satisfied with the Account which *Moses* gives of the Creation, as hitherto it hath been generally understood and received; It much stands them upon, since they reject the *Old*, to find out a *New* and better; which, to give them their due, they do not in the least pretend to, beyond *bare and empty* Conjectures, void of all *Ground and Reason*: Which tho *themselves* may admire, they must allow *others* a due liberty, at the same time, to esteem *ridiculous*.

9. But here, (after this Deviation to return to the matter in hand) we are to take notice that their objected *Pre-Adamitism*, doth not at all prejudice, nor even relate to this Question, which is touching the *Homoniety* of our N ͏s, not their *Origination* or *Descent*. That Creation which they pretend to be *Antecedent*

cedent to *Adam*'s, being, according to the Principles of its firſt Author, no leſs of *Real Men* than this latter; their Poſterity therefore muſt needs be ſuch. And our cauſe hath this further Advantage, that as *Cham's African Race*, and the *Curſe* ſaid to be annexed thereto, do make nothing againſt our *American* (nor yet *Aſian*) Slaves, nor Tributaries; ſo this *Pre-Adamitiſm* doth utterly evacuate and overthrow whatever they from thence might otherwiſe *infer*, tho in it ſelf never ſo concluſive and good.

10. Nor are they like to ſpeed better from the Ninth, than from the three former *Chapters*; unleſs they can make it appear that that Curſe did deprive all *Cham's* Poſterity of their Reaſon, and ſo metamorphoſe them into Brutes. Nor yet even ſo will it do their Work; unleſs they alſo prove that all *Negro's*, whereſoever found, are his Poſterity, and particularly Deſcendents from *Canaan*, againſt whom alone that Curſe was denounced, (as in the progreſs of this Diſcourſe I ſhall ſhew) which will be no very eaſie task. But this I ſhall refer to the next Section to be further conſidered; what at preſent I ſhall think requiſite to be ſpoken being only this, that ſince *Man alone is capable of Diſcipline,* of which our *Negro's,* equally with other People, are : Nothing but Malice can be ſuppoſed to beſpeak them leſs, which even at the ſame time muſt be thought to *bely it ſelf.* And ſo for the preſent letting this and ſuch other Arguments reſt, which they pretend to borrow from the Holy Scripture, where in truth not the leaſt *ſyllable* can be wreſted ſo as to favour this their brutiſh *ſuppoſition*; I ſhall proceed to examine whether the voice of *Reaſon,* the thing they ſo mightily pretend to, will determine more on their behalf, than ether *Religion,* or the *ſacred Writ.*

11. For to do them Right even in this ſo bad a Cauſe, they are not of thoſe who ſhun to anſwer at

this

this Bar, so long as they have any thing which they imagine will make for them, there to be insisted on. But here at last failing, which, 'tis to be presumed, *in such a Case* they cannot but soon do, we may the less blame them, if, for their ultimate refuge and defence, they betake themselves to *Railing,* or even to worse *Arguments.* Their specious *Reasons* on which this pious belief is grounded, do seem to have been drawn from these four *Pretences*; the Complexion, Bondage, Pretended Stupidity, and Barbarousness of our *Negro's* Manners, because different from ours. Of the second of which, they make this *two-fold Use,* first to *Bruti-fie* them; and then, that proving defective, to deprive them of all both *Temporal* and *Spiritual Rights,* which their Manhood, notwithstanding their being Slaves, would otherwise infer : Of which last, I shall speak in its proper place, and in the mean time consider only what relates to the *present* Matter.

12. I shall begin with the first, and that is their *Complexion,* which being most obvious to the sight, by which the *Notion* of things doth seem to be most certainly conveyed to the Understanding, is apt to make no *slight* impressions upon rude Minds, already prepared to admit of any thing for *Truth* which shall make for Interest, especially if supported with but the least *shadow of Argument* : And therefore it may not be so improbable (as I have (elsewhere) heard affirmed) that from so poor a *Medium,* our *Negro's* Brutality should be inferred, by such whose affection to so *gainful* a Doctrine, cannot but make the Way smooth and easie to their Conviction. Such People in these Cases being not apt to reflect, (and, *probably not caring*) how derogatory to the Goodness and *Justice* of God it is, to represent him thus idly Propitious to empty *Shadows,* and even to White and Red, that so out of his infinite regard thereto, he should

throw

throw off all *respect to the Work of his Hand*, and to unman and unsoul so great a part of the Creation: Nor yet, (which is more strange, because their own immediate concern) that the Argument may come one Day to be turned against themselves, and improved to chastise their *Brutishness*, who from thence did at first so maliciously infer that *absurd* Conclusion to the prejudice of so numerous and vast a People.

13. For it is well known, that the *Negro's in their Native Country*, and perhaps here also, if they durst speak their inward *Sentiments*, do entertain as high thoughts of themselves and of their *Complexion*, as our *Europeans* do; and at the same time holding the contrary in an equal disdain, (the like whereof is affirmed of the *Natives of Japan*, as to their own, and the Fashions and Manners of all Strangers, as Mr. *Bloom* in his *Geography* witnesseth): Whereby the *Missionaries of the Roman Church*, (who to facilitate their Conversion, do condescend to humour them in divers things) are said to represent our Blessed Saviour in the *Negro's Complexion*; themselves also describing the *evil Spirit* in ours. Now if Fancy and Opinion against *Reason* must carry it, there is no doubt but they will not spare for that, even to vie with the best of us; and then for number, 'tis certain they can out-muster us. So that without a recourse to Force, the Contest on our part will be managed upon very *unequal terms*, and in no case is like to succeed but to our disadvantage. And for *Force*, I shall in due place shew, how little it can avail in things of this Nature.

14. But the determination of this Point will much depend upon the right understanding and knowledg of *Real Beauty*, a true standard whereof the Nations have not yet pitcht upon. That being Deformity with others, which amongst us is the only *perfect and compleat*

pleat

Pleat Figure. As a certain Author in a *Treatise* upon this Subject, by infinite Collections and Instances in the practice and behaviour of more distant Nations, hath abundantly shewn. So that if the other part of the World should once come to agree upon this particular, without consulting us here (which 'tis possible, when ever they go about it, they may omit), and *like unto us,* maliciously determine the Matter in favour of themselves, they only may be the *Men,* and our selves but *Beasts.*

15. And that no better is like to be the *Issue* of such a Consult, may be from hence concluded, for that the largest proportion of People, perchance five out of six parts of the World, will upon a due survey, be found of a more dull and sable *Complexion* than the *Europeans.* Of whom, as may be probably conjectured, many by mingling with other Nations, as *Spain* with *Moors, Jews* and *Saracens,* are, for the general, short of the *English* clearness. The like may be suspected of other bordering Regions; and of *Britain* it self, if we call to mind the Epithets [*Picti & Cærulei*] which the Poet *Martial, Epig.* 45. *l.* 11. & 99. *l.* 14. bestowed on its Inhabitants. And even of those Countries that are more Northerly, the *Natives* Countenances do differ much from ours. As the swarthy *Americans* about *Hudson's* Bay, and of *Canada,* with the adjacent parts, do testifie. And those of our own Nation, or our Neighbours, who have betaken themselves to these *hotter Climes,* do in a short time after their setting foot here, discover a very discernable alteration, not only from *those at Home,* but from *themselves* also as to what they were at their first arrival. Whose *Off-spring,* after the Succession of some few Ages, may, (judging by what is already visible of many of them) become quite *Black,* at least very *Duskie* and *Brown,* like our brindle *Mulatto's* and *Indians.* The

Persians

Perfians alfo, and *Madagafcars*, with other Eaftern Nations, do carry more fwarthy Complexions, inclining to the *Colour* of the former, and even blacker than the *Moors*: That obfervation of the Poet, *Et mauro obfcurior Indus*; being ftill no lefs true, than when 'twas firft made: Now if the like fhould happen here to our *Englifh Off-fpring*, we fhould one Day have too much caufe to repent of our large Difcoveries in thefe Parts, which of *Men*, (by their being Tranfplanted hither) muft fo inevitably make them to degenerate into Brutes.

16. This Fiction of the Brutality of the *Negro's*, doth contradict that Maxim in common obfervation concerning the *Non-generation* of Monfters; for thefe being no part of the firft Creation, did not obtain from God that Bleffing *of being fruitful and multiplying, and of replenifhing the Earth*, Gen. 1. 28. & 8. 17. which other created Animals then did. According to which our *Mulatto's* and *Meftizo's* (the production of *Negro* or *Indian mixtures*, with other lefs fwarthy People) would want this prolific faculty, and never be able to *procreate their like*; the contrary whereof is daily feen in this and in the other *Colonies*. The like alfo would be the condition of the *African Moors*, oppofite to *Spain* and *Italy*, of whom 'tis fcarce to be doubted but that they are a mixt Generation; defcendents of *Negro's*, the firft Inhabitants, and *Europeans*, from the oppofite Shores, by whofe People they have formerly been Conquered; Their Hair, Figure, and Complexion (the fame with our *Mulatto's*) befpeaking no lefs. Whereas our remoter *Africans*, into whofe Territories thofe Nations never till of late had pierced, and fo had no opportunity of the like Mixtures, are perfectly Black, their Hair frizled like Wooll, as the many thoufands here do witnefs. Now all thefe *Moors*, muft, *like the Mules* (from whom the term *Mulatto* is borrowed) be for ever Barren, admitting the faid Suppofition and Maxim to be alike true. 17. Here-

17. Herein doth also concur every Man's Senſe and Judgment touching other Creatures, nothing doubted (tho *Black*) to be of the ſame *ſpecies*, with the *Whiter:* As is ſeen of Birds, which do often differ much in the Feather, yet neverthelefs are one and the ſame in kind. But, alas! for this the poor *African* muſt be Unman'd and Unſoul'd ; accounted, and even ran-ked with *Brutes.* A partiality highly becoming Chri-ſtians, pretending to ſo much Juſtice and Knowledg, which ſome do arrogate to themſelves, and would even be thought to profeſs, whilſt they practice and aſſert Principles ſo oppoſite ther eunto !

18. Here alſo it might be demanded, Why *Colours* ſhould do more than *Deformities*, by all granted not to prejudice the concerned party as to his *Species* ? A Crooked Perſon, Dwarf, or Hermophrodite , being as truly of the *Species* of Man, as any the more Com-pleat, Simple, and well Proportioned. The Canons of the *Church* formerly (and for ought appears ſtill) allowing even thoſe laſt, as capable of Benefices with-out Diſpenſation, ſaith one, and to be promoted to *Holy Orders.* And both the *Civil* and *Common Law* not prohibiting them to be inſtituted Heirs, to ſuc-cced to an Inheritance. And even Monſtrous Births partaking of Mankind, having the benefit and help of Reaſon, may very well, ſaith the ſame Perſon, be ad-mitted to ſucceed to their Parents *dying Inteſtate,* ac-cording to the cuſtom of moſt Countries, which wil-leth that the *Dead* ſhould give *Seizin* to the *Living.*

19. To this, I ſhall not think it time miſpent to re-hearſe a Story, borrowed out of a *French* Author made *Engliſh* ; which happened, as he ſaith, not many years ſince, near *Argenton*, a Town in *Normandy.* It is this : `` A certain Gentleman complotted with ſome Neigh-`` bours there to play certain Plays, wherein ſhould be `` acted certain *Devils*, to the intent that the Pleaſure `` and

" and Paftime of their *Pageant* might be greater. And
" this Gentleman would needs himfelf be attired in
" the habit of a *Devil*, and did perfonate fuch a part ;
" Infomuch, as after the Plays were ended, he chafed
" in his Furniture, went home to his *Wife*, and had
" company with her clad in the fame attire wherein
" he *played the Devil*. By means whereof, fhe at the
" end of nine Months, was delivered of a *Son* fo
" Monftrous, as in his Countenance, Head, Face, and
" all the parts of his Body, efpecially in his Feet, he
" refembled and was more like unto a *Satyr*, fuch as
" the Poets have defcribed, than unto an ordinary and
" natural Man.   After this he had other Children ; all
" which, together with their brother the *Monfter*, did
" furvive both their Parents.   Upon whofe deceafe
" there grew a Contention and Variance between them,
" touching the *fucceffion* of his Inheritance ; all of them
" endeavouring to exclude this Monfter, not only from
" the birth-right of being Heir and Eldeft Son, but
" even from the total *Succeffion* of any thing that he
" fhould claim, that might in Right appertain unto
" him.   Hereupon was the Procefs fued , and the
" Matter proceeded in fuit between them, before a
" Judge of an *Inferiour Court* : By whom it was or-
" dered that they fhould make their Entry upon the
" *Eftate*, and that the Eldeft Brother fhould Inherit,
" as next Heir to his Parents, according to the Cu-
" ftom of *Normandy*.   From this Sentence, the youn-
" ger Brethren brought their Appeal , and removed
" the Suit into the Court of *Parliament* of *Roan*, where
" it was by them pleaded, that he was a very Mon-
" fter born, and that there was no Reafon that he
" fhould be accounted a *Man*. But hereunto it was
" replied, *That thofe were not in any fort to be allowed*
" *Monfters, who are born of Mankind, and are capable of*
" *Reafon, and of the future Refurreƈion*. But thofe
" only

" only are to be held for such, who are born of some
" *Beaft*, and not of a Man ; which laft, as they are
" forthwith to be flain, fo the former may not in any
" fort be fo dealt with, *whether they have the ufe of Rea-*
" *fon or not* ; but be fo Monftrous as not having fo
" much as the Face of a Man, but rather of fome
" Beaft. Nor are they ever denied due fucceffion in
" Inheritance ; but the Monfter doth either Bellow
" like an Ox, or eat Grafs as a Sheep, *performing only*
" *the actions of a Beaft.*   And therefore the Defendents
" concluded, that the Judgment had been *well and*
" *rightly yielded :* And the Court by a folemn Arreft,
" did confirm the fame, and pronounce that the Sen-
" tence, from which the Brethren had Appealed, *fhould*
" *be fully and wholly Executed,* &c.   Thus far our Author. Wherein may be obferved, that as *Intereft* induced the younger Brethren to confpire together to deprive the Elder of his Inheritance upon the advantage
of his Deformity, fo the *Reafons and Arguments* ufed
in his behalf, together with the *Sentence* thereupon a-
warded. do prove as much for our *Negro's*, as for that
fuppofed *Monfter*.   To this I fhall add, that in the
Book before mentioned (*Numb.* 14. of this Section)
confifting of ftrange Reprefentations and unufu-
al *Features*, both of Face and Body , agreeable to
the Fafhions and *Cuftoms* of the feveral places they relate unto, but much exceeding the *deformity of Com-*
plexion ; the Author doth not therefore in the leaft feem
to fufpect any of them, as if thereby the further removed from *perfect and real Men.*

20. This opinion alfo, if driven to the head, would
infer another no lefs ftrange and before unheard of
conceit in Divinity, *viz. That Colours are a means of*
Grace, and have a power in them to *recommend us to*
God.   Whence it would follow, that Vertue fhould be
an unfeparable attendant upon Beauty ; and the faireft
Bodies

Bodies muſt then inevitably inſhrine the pureſt and brighteſt Souls; the contrary whereto was the Satyriſt's obſervation. The holy Scripture no leſs informing us the ſame, when it teacheth us, that God looks not upon *the Countenance, or the height of the Stature, nor ſeeth as Man ſeeth, but God looks upon the Heart.* And in truth, this whole Argument is fraught with too many evil Conſequences and Abſurdities to be relied on : and therefore deſerves to be thrown aſide, and be forgotten into a diſuſe, as too dangerous a Weapon for Slaves to learn the uſe of from us. And which being turned to the other end, may be ſo improved as to humble us to the ſame *Brutality*, which we ſo ridiculouſly have imputed to our *Negro's.*

21. NOR will *Bondage*, which is the next thing to be treated of, do any more towards this Metamorphoſing and Brutifying of our *Negro's*, than Deformities could : It being not to be imagined by ſober Men (whatever the diſtracted Tribe may do) that Misfortunes and evil *Accidents* ſhould carry that force in them as to alter Subſtances; there being no ſo great Faſcinations attending the mightieſt changes of Fortune, as thereby to take away the nature of things. For he that before was a Rich Man, or Potentate, is ſtill a Man, tho like *Belizarius,* become a Beggar. *Marius* was as much a Man when conceiled in the Marſh and Dungeon, as when he arrived to be *Conſul* the Seventh time. And *Cæſar* when in the Pirats hands, was the ſame Man, as when he got to be Perpetual *Dictator.* *David* was but a Man when he was King of *Iſrael*; and ſo he was too, when purſued by *Saul.* Nor did *Job* become a Beaſt upon his great Loſſes, any more than he could be ſuppoſed more than a Man, upon his *Reſtauration.* Now Slavery is but a lower degree of Poverty and Miſery; but not the loweſt; for there are conditions more Calamitous; As to be

be deprived of all the Comforts of Life by a perpetual Confinement and Neceſſity, with a continual
dread and expectation of a miſerable Death. So alſo
to be vexed with loathſome Ulcers, and ſharp tormenting Diſeaſes, all hopes of Relief and Reſpite being
cut off; are conditions to which Slavery, ſimply and
alone, is to be preferred. Yet none of theſe do unman the Party, tho they may much humble and de-
baſe him. Such evils altering only the *outward ſtate* of
things, but making no impreſſion upon the *inner Man*,
further than as our ſelves ſhall give way thereto;
which froward and impatient Minds can as well do
without it. An adverſe Fortune may deprive us of
our Goods and Liberty, but not of our Souls and Reaſon. Of which whilſt we are poſſeſſed, and do quietly
enjoy, 'tis neither the Ambition nor Covetouſneſs, much
leſs the Frowns and Menaces of any Imperious or *Ty-
rannic Lord*, can bereave us of that *Right* which we
naturally have to be ranked within the Degree and
Species of Men.

22. And to manifeſt this, I will ſuppoſe, what I
would be loth ſhould happen, that ſome one of this
Iſland going for *England*, ſhould chance to be ſnapt
by an *Algerine*, or *Corſaire* of *Barbary*, and there to be
ſet on Shore and Sold; Doth he thereupon become a
Brute? If not, why ſhould an *African*, (ſuppoſe of
that, or any other remote part) ſuffer a greater alteration than one of us? This certainly muſt either not be,
or muſt proceed from ſome ſecret power peculiar to
that Soil and Air, where Slaves are gendred and made;
and then what Spell have we againſt ſuch powerful and
ſtrange *Brute-Anthropies?*

23. If Slavery had that force or power ſo as to unſoul Men, it muſt needs follow, that every great Con-
queror might at his pleaſure, make and unmake Souls;
and a Servant running away, or buying his Freedom,
would

would make himself one : As on the contrary, he that suffered *his Ears to be boared at his Master's Door-post*, Exod. 21. 6. must in that act annihilate and destroy his Soul, his Body nevertheless surviving. And the having, or not having of a Soul, would signifie but the bare enjoyment or want of *Liberty*; of which a *Horse* is no less capable than a *Man*.

24. But that Conquest and Subjection can make no impression upon the Soul, is plain even from this, that it cannot effect a less thing; *not subdue the Will*, which yet is under the command of the Soul, but not within the *Adversaries* power: A Victory being rarely heard of which makes the *Affections* to yield, and reduceth the Will of the conquered Party : as the Poet long since sang;

——— *Victoria nulla est,*
Quam quæ confessos animo quoq; subjugat hostes.

Now Religion being, according to *Lactantius*, of *all things most Voluntary*, cannot be expelled its hold at another's pleasure ; nay, it is not under the power of the *Owner* ; for a Man cannot believe, or not believe whatever he pleaseth. Now all that can be said to abate the power of *Conquest* over the Will or Mind, doth conclude more strongly against our *Plagiaries*, who are invested with a less full and compleat Authority over their *Captives* and Slaves, then Conquerors are.

25. And here withall it might be considered, how monstrous and inhumanly cruel they are, who do both buy and retain in this *Soul-murthering and Brutifying-state of Bondage*, those whom they might so easily restore to their pristine *Homoneity*, and of meer Beasts, with one little blast of their Mouths, even but a word or two, convert into Men ; and be at the same time the

the happy *Authors* of life to Souls, as well as freedom to Bodies. A Privilege too great and glorious for the reft of the World to enjoy, and yet *not regarded here.*

26. Again, If Slavery hath such a faculty or power as to tranfmute Men into Beafts, or if all *Negro's* be naturally such, may we not be bold to demand what will become of thofe *Debauches,* that fo frequently do make ufe of them for their *unnatural* Pleafures and Lufts? Or of fuch of our People, who have Intermarried with them ? Sure they would be loth to be endited of *Sodomy,* as for lying with a Beaft, It would be therefore convenient for them to renounce that Beaftly opinion ; or elfe that the Law may have its free Courfe, and *be let loofe upon them :* Of which they would have no caufe to complain, but of that firft wicked Principle.

27. Laftly, If a Slave fetting foot upon the Soil of fome Countries, (as of *France*) be thereby at the very inftant made a *Freeman* ; or elfe, (as in the fame Kingdom is alfo cuftomary) *by receiving Baptifm :* It muft needs follow that thefe feveral Actions have the faculty to tranfubftantiate Things and Perfons : becaufe by fetting Slaves at Liberty, they furnifh them with Souls ; and of certain Creatures, of a different *Species,* (for that will neceffarily follow, if they were not fuch before) *do create them Men.* But, if this be falfe, then being become free, they either muft ftill be *without Souls,* or elfe were induced therewith in their very Slavery ; the latter of which muft needs be true, the firft being not in the leaft fufpected.

28. And here alfo it may be demanded and confidered, why Liberty and Freedom fhould effect more upon *Men,* than upon other *Creatures* ; who according to this Suppofition, the *wilder* they are, becaufe thereby the more at *Liberty,* would fo much the nearer

approach

approach to *Humanity*, and be endued with Souls too ; But (which of all the reſt, is moſt Monſtrous) with ſuch Souls, as muſt in all things agree with an *Animal*, or Brutiſh (not a *Rational*) being, tho tranſ-formed into Men. And ſo all Subiects and ſubordinate *Governors* would be Men but in part ; but yet by ſo much the more, by how much they approached nearer to *Abſoluteneſs*. And in all the *Grand Seignior's* ſpaci-ous Dominions, where there are none but Slaves, there would not be ſo much as one Man beſides himſelf ; not excepting the very *Chriſtians*. The evil conſe-quences of which Belief, the *Authors* thereof may ſooner feel, than they are willing to underſtand or ſee.

29. There were no Men in the World ſo likely as the ancient *Greeks* and *Romans*, to have entertained this baſe eſteem of Slaves ; becauſe void of all impe-diments to their Senſuality, and free from thoſe ties of Conſcience unto which *Chriſtianity* is ſubject, had they had any colour of Reaſon for it ; and, being ſuch from whom are tranſmitted to us the greateſt preſi-dents of Severity towards their *Slaves*, as having no Reſtraints beſides the goodneſs of their Diſpoſition and *Genius*, which were not always very operative in di-vers of them ; yet Reaſon prevailed ſo far with them, as to confeſs them to be Men, nothing appearing upon *Record* in contradiction thereto, but very much from their *Poets* and *Writers* in the confirmation of it. Hence that trite Diſtich, aſcribed to *Cato*, adviſeth, *Sî fueris ſervos mercatus, &c. Homines tamen eſſe memento*. Agreeable to that of the *Greek* Poet *Philemon*, thus ex-preſſing the ſame Article of the *Gentiles* Belief ; Κὰν δ̔ ᾖ τις, ὀδὲν ἧττον, δέσποτα, Ἄνθρωπος ᾧος ἐσίν, &c. *That is, That no one is the leſs a Man for Servitude*. And no leſs doth the good natured Maſter in *Juvenal* acknowledg, when on his Slaves behalf he delivers

this

this Oracle, *Nulla unquam de morte hominis cunctatio longa*. That no confideration could be too great where a Man's Life (then, as is faid, pleading for his Slave) was concerned. Which the Virago Miftrefs in her Reply, durft not Contradict, *O Demens! Ita Servus Homo eft?* Tho fhe derided her Husbands tendernefs. And *Auguftus Cæfar*, as I think *Dion* relates of him, being invited to a Dinner, where he overheard the outcrys of a certain Slave, condemned to be Impaled for a mifcarriage about fome Criftal Glaffes, forbad the Execution, affirming, *That the Life of a Man (that is, of that Slave) was of too great value to be deftroyed for Trifles.* And *Tully*, fpeaking of Juftice, declares it due, *Etiam adverfus Infimos*, even to the bafeft fort of Men, which he there affirms Slaves to be. And tho thefe Heathens did not much trouble their Slaves with Religion, yet their allowing it to them (which thefe words of *Ariftophanes*, in his *Acharneif. pag. 572* where he introduceth one, ευδαιμονει τον βιον, *Deacum fervulis facrificantem*, as the Paraphraft reades it (The fame δουετης being ufed *Ecclef. το. 651* in oppofition to ελευθερος,) do not obfcurely intimate, doth plainly difcover in what rank of Creatures they accounted them. And for the *Jews* and *Turks*, their being admitted to the Paffeover, *Exod. 12* by the *Britifh* and the others real to profelyte Slaves, both *Negro'd* and others, do teftifie the free of them. And even the laft, who under the like temptation of *Profpority* do not think it worth the giving the Lye fo palpably to both their own and every Man's Reafon.

§. 30. THE two laft things objected, are the *Negro's Stupidity*, and the pretended *barbaroufnefs* of their Manners, both which, for brevity, I fhall difpatch together. Their Barbaroufnefs (which I fhall treat of firft) muft be difcernable either in their Demeanour and Converſation in the World, or elſe from their behaviour and practice in their *Worſhip* and *Cere-monies* of *Religion*; or from both. Now for Religion, It cannot be denied but that nothing is more barbarous, and contrary to Chriſtianity, than their *Polygamy,* their *Idolatrous Dances,* and *Revels*; in which they uſually ſpend the *Sunday* after that the neceſſity of labour for their Proviſions (for the Planting of which, that Day alone is allotted them) has been complied with. But as to theſe, the blame doth lie wholly upon ſuch, who pretending themſelves Chriſtians, do ſuffer and even compel them to thoſe Actions; part whereof are againſt their Wills, and where even a Check or Frown, would reſtrain them from the reſt.

31. And here, that I may not be thought too raſh-ly to impute Idolatry to their *Dances,* my Conjecture is raiſed upon this ground (beſides their being *Gen-tiles*), for that they uſe their Dances as a *means to pro-cure Rain:* Some of them having been known to beg this Liberty upon the Week Days, in order there-unto. Now it is certain, that the *Gentiles* anciently did eſteem and practiſe *Dancing,* as a part of *Divine Worſhip:* And no leſs alſo did the *Jews*; as may be proved from *Exod.* 32. 19. and from *David's Dancing before the Ark,* 2 Sam. 6. Add to this their placing confidence in certain Figures, and ugly Repreſentati-ons, of none knows what beſides themſelves (wh.ch very decently for want of more *Magnificent Temples,* they uſually enſhrine in ſome ſtately *Earthen Potſherds,*) The Fugitives and Runaways believing theſe *Deities* able to protect them in their Flight, and from Diſco-very, (like as the *Egyptians* worſhiping of *Baal Zephon,* was to detect them): Their companions and fellow Slaves alſo, that remain'd at Home, having been over-heard upon the ſeizure of theſe *Puppets,* in a ſearch after the other, inſtantly to give aſſurance that there

D was

was no poſſibility of their further concealment. And
this doubtleſs is a manifeſt token of their *Impiety* in this
kind, and no leſs of their *Barbarity.* But as Chriſtianity would ſoon (*if duly applied*) cure this evil ;
ſo I ſee not how it ſhould prove them to be Brutes,
more than the reſt of the World, formerly, and even
to this Day, more or leſs, addicted to the ſame vanity
and deception of *falſe Worſhip.*

32. And then as to their *Civil* Converſation and
outward Demeanour in the World, it cannot be expected it ſhould be ſo Gentile and Modiſh as our *Europeans,* who perchance muſt be acknowledged as not to
be parallel'd by any other of the three Quarters thereof ; upon whom yet as great Barbarity was formerly
no leſs chargeable ; as moſt *Authors* do agree. *Plutarch,*
in the Life of *Theſeus,* tells us that the *Athenians* lived
ſcattering like the wild *Nomades* of *Scythia,* before
they were by him reduced to a better order of Life,
formed into civil Societies, and acquainted with the
bleſſings of Government. And the *Aborigines* are by
Saluſt, deſcribed to have been, *Genus hominum agreſte,
ſine legibus, ſine imperio, liberum atque ſolutum ;* Certain wild People, without Laws, or Government, looſe
and deſtitute of all poſitive Obligations. And *Ceſar's*
account of the Ancient *Britains,* is not ſuch as ſhould
make us proud ; For he informs us that they were clad
with Skins, and did paint their Bodies ; (from which
cuſtom the name of *Britain* is by our *Cambden* derived). He alſo adds, that *Brothers* with Brothers, and
Parents with their Children, had Wives in common :
A greater Barbarity than I have at any time heard of
amongſt the *Negro's.* And this we find, of them,
very late, and but a few Years before our *Saviours*
Birth, tho ſituated much nearer to the civilized World,
and withal in a colder Clime, than any part of *Africa,*
and moſt of *America.* And ſo little were they advanced

ced in Civility by their converſe with a gentiler People, that even two hundred Years after this entrance
of *Cæſar*, we find the forementioned *Epithets* of
[*Picti* and *Cerulei*] continued to them. Nor doth
Tacitus give any more honourable account of the *Ger-
mans*, from whom the *Saxons*, our immediate Anceſtors are ſprung. Of whoſe Barbarouſneſs alſo *Gildas*
a *Britain*, with other of our Writers, have delivered
no very creditable Account. The *Danes*, who ſupplan-
ted them, were full as bad, if not worſe. And the
Picts who inhabited the North of *Britain*, had that
Name continued long after the other had loſt it;
for no better Reaſon than that, for which the firſt had
it given them. Neither is it improbable but that the
Gaities and Adornments of Elder Ages, did much
conſiſt in Diſcolouring and Painting themſelves, which
is ſtill practiſed in *America*. Our greater Perſonages
no leſs affecting the like diverſity of Colours in their
Attire; and yet muſt be reputed (not *Barbarous*, but)
Gentile for it. The like Cuſtom 'tis poſſible was in uſe
amongſt other Nations, were their *Antiquities* raked
into. And tho *Ireland* in times paſt, as is intimated
by *V. Bede, Eccl. Angl Hiſt. l. 3. c. 24. & 47.* be re-
ported to have been a place of Learning, ſo that other
Countries are ſaid to have ſent their *Youth* thither, as
to another *Greece*, or *Athens*, to be trained up in Learning; yet ſo much are they Degenerated, or at leaſt ſo
little Fruit thereof hath of late accrued to their Poſterity, that the *Natives* of that Kingdom, who have
been Imported hither, are obſerved to be, in divers re-
ſpects, more Barbarous than the *Negro's*: And this in
its kind is ſo notorious in ſome of them, as to fall under even the *Negro's* obſervation; by whom this petu-
lent Taunt hath contemptuouſly, and in reproach
of their doltiſh Stupidity, been returned upon them,
viz. "*That if the Iriſhman's Country had firſt lighted in*

the

" *the Englishman's way, he might have gone no further*
" *to look for Negro's* : That is, Slaves, such as the Negro's here generally are. (These two words, *Negro*
and *Slave*, being by custom grown Homogene-
ous and Convertible ; even as *Negro* and *Christian*,
Englishman and *Heathen*, are by the like corrupt Custom and Partiality made *Opposites* ; thereby as it were
implying, that the one could not be *Christians*, nor the
other *Infidels*.)

33. Which Indication of our *Negro's* contempt of
that dull and flegmatick People, doth shew the cause
of their Ignorance to be the want of Converse and
Education, which may also befal other Nations, and
even the Inhabitants of our *Mother Country*. It being
certain, that *Africa* was once famous for both Arts and
Arms ; that *Carthage* did rival with *Rome* for the
World's Empire, and had well nigh gotten it, tho
now become an *Aceldama* of Barbarism ; even to the
degree of rendring its Inhabitants suspected for Brutes,
as we here find and see. And it is also evident, that
all our own People do not exceed these either for
Knowledg, or *Piety* ; nor yet always for *Civility*, whatsoever Brutishness is by some proudly objected to them.
And without a provision for Schools (of which the
scattering way of living in these *Colonies* is scarce capable) together with a stricter Care taken to suppress
Debauchery (hardly to be outdone (therein) by *Sodom*,
were it standing) may at last end in the like Barbarity ;
and like that lasting monument of God's Wrath against
Impiety, may, without a timely Repentance and Reformation, be made a like Spectacle and Example to
such as desire to live ἀσεβεῖς *without Religion, suffering
for it the vengeance of Eternal Fire.*

34. But in our own People, neither their *Ignorance*, nor *Vicious Lives*, nor any never so barbarous
Practices, doth render their being Men the more suspected ;

spected ; nor cause any question touching their *Right
to Religion, tho not at all prized by them.* Which yet is
plainly upon pretence thereof (how justly I shall else-
where discover) denied even to the *Infants* of the
other, tho their Parents, or at least one of them, were
Baptized, and (according to that measure of Knowledg they had attained to) *Professors of Christianity*;
it may be imported out of *England.* For even of those
they take no more care ; Nor yet of such other, whom
themselves, tho but *seldom* (yet *sometimes*) have for fashion sake, upon their being there, caused to be *Baptized :* I say, even to these, they permit the exercise
of *Religion,* ro otherwise, then as they do to the
most *Ignorant* of them.   But rather upon their return,
untwisting as it were that *Web,* they seemed to
weave in *England.* Remitting them to their former
Stations, and compelling them to herd it with their
wilder Countrymen, and as it were forcing them to
revive their Paganism. Not allowing their Children
Baptism; nor suffering them upon better terms *than
direct Fornication,* to live with their Women (for Wives
I may not call them, being never Married).   And accounting it Foppish, when Dead, to think of giving
them *Christian,* or even decent Burial ; that so their
pretence for Brutifying them, might find no Contradiction.

35. Nor would I be thought to speak this at Random.   For I cannot easily forget the *supercilious* Checks
and *Frowns* (to say no worse), which I have upon this
occasion alone met with ; and for such innocent Arguments and Persuasions, I have, in the opinion of some
chill Professors (otherwise called *Atheists*), perhaps less
prudently, (*I am sure to the Ruine of my small Interest*)
been sometimes bold to urge to our People, in order
to their Conviction, as to the *necessity of this Duty,*
Particularly once, soon after my arrival into this new

D 3   World,

World, for minding a *Negro* of his *Baptifmal Vow* formerly made in *England*, not doubting it to be grateful to his Mafter, whom I took for a difcreet *Perfon:* Which indeed·he was, fo far as getting of Money, *quo* ~~mdll~~, *quáque injuriâ*, would amount to; in which his Wifdom, I afterward found, did wholly confift. By others it hath been demanded of me, *What I had to do with their Servants*, when once affirming them to be a part of a *Minifter*'s Care and Charge. Another time it was told me with no fmall *Paffion* and Vehemency, and that by a *Religious* Perfon (for fo in all things elfe fhe appeared), that I might as well Baptize a Puppy, as a certain young *Negro*, the Mother whereof was a *Chriftian*, and for ought I know (notwith-ftanding her Complexion) *as dear to God as her felf.* Nor was this Gentlewoman in the leaft infected with *Anabaptifm*, but a frequenter of the Church, and very carefully procuring always for her own, what fhe thus denied to her *Negro's* Children. And another of the *fame Sex*, upon my baptizing a *Male Negro* of hers, of about thirty Years old, fpeaking *Englifh* plainly, and earneftly befeeching it; caufed this Meffage to be deli-vered to me, That *Baptifm, I was to· underftand, was to one of thofe no more beneficial, than to her black Bitch.* Others alfo of both *Sexes*, I have heard *Scof-fing* and inveighing at it, with no little fpite and inve-teracy; tho not appearing fuch, whom I might take for abfolute *enemies to Religion*; which I fear too many, in thefe parts, are. And in truth, the hard Words, and evil Language I have upon this account received (and do expect will now *again be repeated*) would take up too much room here to be rehearfed; nor is it very pleafant for me to remember, further than to blame that firft *horrid Principle*, the natural refult whereof thefe Difcourfes and Practices have moft certainly been. " There being no doubt but that (to ufe the words

" of

" of one of our *Homilies*, in an almoſt parallel caſe)
" they take the multitude [of *Negro's,* I ſhall add]
" for vile Souls, of whoſe loſs and ſafeguard no Re-
" putation is to be had ; for whom yet Chriſt payed as
" dearly, as for the mightieſt Prince, or the wiſeſt and
" beſt learned in the Earth. And they that will have
" it generally taken for indifferent, that a very few
" take no hurt (herein alone the Caſe differs, all
" being involved in the ſame Neglect and Dan-
" ger) tho infinit multitudes beſides periſh thereby,
" do ſhew that they put little difference between the
" Multitude and brute Beaſts, whoſe danger they ſo
" little eſteem. And in this belief, I am the ſtronger
confirmed, for that ſome of them are more *indifferent,*
as to the baptizing of their *Mulatto's,* as conceiving
theſe a leſs degree removed from *Men,* whoſe Parents
on the one ſide are *Engliſh,* or of the *Whiter ſort* ;
whilſt to ſuch as are wholly the Off-ſpring of *Negro's,*
they utterly deny it.

36. I am not ignorant but that upon the diſperſing and publiſhing of theſe Diſcourſes (if ever ſuch a thing ſhould happen) the Correſpondents and *Factors* for our People reſiding in *England,* (no leſs than thoſe here) diſliking to ſee their *myſtery of Iniquity* laid open to the view of the World, may be apt (as moſt certainly they will) to decry the whole charge as a piece of *Calumny* and *Slander* ; notwithſtanding that their Practice is ſo notorious, and there is no one, not per-

Since the committing of theſe Papers to the Preſs, even while the laſt ſheet was Printing, a certain Berbadian *openly maintained theſe Poſitions , That* Negro's *were Beaſts , and had no more Souls than Beaſts, and that Religion did not concern them. Adding that they went not to thoſe parts to ſave Souls, or propagate Religion , but to get Money. Which, with much more to the ſame purpoſe ,he uttered with ſo much paſſion and vehemency, that all who heard him, believ'd he ſpake not more his own, than the ſenſe and opinion of the place.*

fectly

fectly *blind*, that can avoid the seeing of it; *Nay, even such cannot but know it.* Which must be granted by all to arise either from *Infidel Paganism*, with a Contempt, and even renouncing of the *Gospel* of our LORD (which is much the worst); or from that other of their conceiving their *Negro's* to be but Brutes. Unto which last, their Discourse doth rather encline, tho there be no small cause for suspicion also of the first. Others again may hope to *shelter* themselves under that *common subterfuge for Blasphemies*, That what of this kind hath at any time escaped them, was only to sharpen their Understandings and Wits, by thus whetting them *with Dispute*; or else that they uttered nothing further than by way of *Railery*. For my part, I shall not presume to dive into their *Intentions*, nor judg of their Thoughts; but only beg this kindness of them, That if I must take their Arguments for *feigned*, they would favour me so far as to suppose the same of my *Answers*; and withal accept of this further Advice, viz. *Not to practise Opinions, which they are ashamed to own amongst better People.* It being most certain, that what elsewhere they would perchance have thought to be Dispute only, and *in jest*, is here acted in the *strictest earnest*; even beyond the equity of their *Hypothesis*, treating their Slaves with far less Humanity than they do their *Cattel*. For they do not use to *starve* their Horse, which they expect shall both carry and credit them upon the Road; nor to *pinch the Cow* of her Fodder, by whose Milk their *Families* are sustained: Which yet (to their *eternal* shame) is too frequently the lot and condition of these *poor People*, from whose labour their Wealth and *Livelihoods* do wholly arise: But yet, *whose possessours* [whilst they] *slay* [and starve] *them*, (not only their Souls but their Bodies also, which are worn out in perpetual Toil for them) *do* nevertheless *hold themselves not guilty*; and they

they that Sell them say, Bleſſed be the Lord, for I am rich; and *their own Shepherds pity them not;* as the Prophet *Zechariah* ſpeaks. A Cruelty capable of no Palliation, and for which *Vengeance* cannot be long expected ere it fall upon the *inhumane Authors.* Nor to ſpeak truth, without that πρῶτον ψεῦδος of their *Negro's* brutality, do I ſee how thoſe other *Inhumanities,* as their Emaſculating and Beheading them, their *croping off their Ears* (which they uſually cauſe the Wretches to broyl, and then compel to eat them themſelves); their *Amputations of Legs,* and even Diſſecting them alive; (this laſt I cannot ſay was ever practiſed, but has been certainly affirmed by ſome of them, as no leſs allowable than to a Beaſt, of which they did not in the 'eaſt doubt but it was juſtifiable). Add to this their *ſcant allowance* for Clothes, as well as Diet, and (which is often the calamity of the *moſt Innocent and Labourious*) their no leſs working than ſtarving them to Death; all which could never otherwiſe be ſo glibly ſwallowed by them, but upon a *perſuaſion* of this, or of the former worſe Principle. Both without doubt contrived in Hell, receiving their firſt impreſſions in no other than the *Devil's Mint,* purpoſely deſigned for the *murthering* of Souls; Invented only *to defeat the Mercies of God in their bleſſed Redeemer,* and to render void and ineffectual his precious Blood ſhed upon the *Croſs,* for the ſaving of the World. And thus much ſhall ſuffice for proof of the *Antecedent* of my ſecond Propoſition, deduced from my firſt general *Aſſertion.*

§. III. 1. My *Antecedent* being thus made evident, I ſhall betake my ſelf to conſider the *Conſequent, viz.* Of the *Right* which our *Negro's* have, and may juſtly claim to the exerciſe of *Religion,* upon the truth of what hath been ſaid touching their being *Men.* A
thing

thing that of it self, one would think should naturally follow, and be granted even of course; did not the *Adversaries* thereto hope, tho our *Antecedent* were acknowledged, yet notwithstanding this by some other ways, to invalidate this *Right*, and to continue them Heathens. In *order* whereto, they are not wanting of a twofold Argument; First, The *Imprecation of Noah:* Secondly, Their forfeiture of this *Right* by Servitude. Now as before, they imployed the first to unman their *Negro's*; so, that failing, here they no less generously *wrest* it to rob them of *Religion* (no less than of all other Rights): An *injury* (as in the end I shall shew) far exceeding the former, of making them *Brutes* simply, and abstracted from the latter.

2. Before I shall go about to answer which, I shall desire the Reader to *remark* that what they have hitherto urged, is only against the *Christianizing of Negro's*, with such only of other Nations and Complexions who are under Bondage: Bearing it in hand (be like) that the condition of the *Tributary Indians* upon the Continent, of *Hostages of Peace* delivered up to the *English* upon the *Public Faith*, or of the *Manumissed* and freed Slaves, whether from *Persia, Madagascar*, or the *East* and *West Indies*, brought hither, (none of them likely, *especially the last*, to have been descendants from *Cham*, any more than our selves;) enjoyed amongst them a more happy and blessed state, as to Religion. Which in truth they cannot affirm even of such of them, who do live in their *Families* in the nature of Hirelings; nor of their *Neighbours*, whose Habitations are invironed by the *English*. Who yet have been accountable upon all occasions for Taxes; even as the *Hostages* before mentioned have been (like Bondmen and Captives) strictly kept to Labour, by those to whose care they were committed for *Education* and *Security* of the *Peace*; which certainly had been

the

the most effectual way to disturb it, had their Relations and Friends been *strong* enough. To whose *Temper* and *Disposition*, nothing is more contrary then hard Labour, nor esteemed so *miserable* a condition; which the Parents tears (one whereof was a *Werrowanza*, that is, a *Toparch*, or *Royetlet* of the place; and the rest his principal great Men) shed at the view thereof, did sufficiently evidence.

3. And so betaking my self to the first Objection, which certainly is their *chief strength*; I shall consider these People as *Negro's*, abstracted from their condition of Bondage, and only as *Natives* of *Africa*, at least Originally; believed to be Descendants from *Cham*, and under the *Curse*, as is pretended; which is all we shall speak of in this place; reserving their Condition to be discoursed of alone, and by it self, in the ensuing Section.

4. And here, in the first place, I cannot but take notice, that this Objection is founded on a *Supposition*, including in it these five *Falshoods*, or (at best) *Uncertainties*. 1. That the *Negro's* are of *Cham's* Race. 2. That both *Cham* and his *whole Posterity* were under the *Curse*. 3. That this *Curse* was in its effects to be *perpetual*, even to the last Generation. 4. That it extended to their *very Souls*, and was a kind of *Reprobation*. 5. That this is a sufficient Ground not only for *enslaving* them, but for keeping them from the exercise of *Religion*. Nothing of which last can possibly from thence be deduced; nor even the former of *enslaving* them; unless, after the rest is proved, they make this appear also; that we are the *Brethren*, whom they were to serve; and that the *Curse* did confer on us a full and perfect *Right of Dominion* them.

5. However, to make out the first, they tell us (or at least do insinuate) that *Noah* and his Sons descending
ing

ing from the *Ark*, did, as it were all upon the suddain (as if afraid of each other), instantly retire into the most *distant parts* of the World (for so *Guinea* is to Mount *Ararat*); of whom *Cham* directed his course to *Africa*, his Posterity the *Negro's* (they are sure) there keeping possession till this very Day, notwithstanding the great *alterations* elsewhere.

6. But to answer this: First, It is wholly improbable that *Noah's* Sons should make any such separation, before being bescanted of Room, they found it necessary to remove; not, 'tis to be presumed, so far as they would go, but some *convenient distance* only, for their better Accommodation; which doubtless they might find, before they had crost all *Africa*.

7. But secondly, Supposing both to have happened, yet 'tis not likely, *at least* not certain, that his Posterity have kept possession there ever since, and that upon the Reasons before mentioned, *viz.* The Possibility of being removed and driven thence back again by *Invasion* and *Conquest*; by none less to be suspected or questioned, than by us here in *America*, to whom it is evident how little security against such alterations, the *Remoteness* of places have been. So that the present Inhabitants of *Africa*, (even that supposure of *Cham's* Race seating there being granted) might have as little Relation to its first *Seaters* and *Planters*, as the *Spaniards*, or our selves, had to the *Natives* here; the *Saxons* to the *Britains*, or the old *Romans* to the *Aborigines*.

8. Thirdly, This, as to a great part of it, is not only *uncertain* and *unlikely*, but *plainly false*. For in an Account we meet with in the holy *Scripture* (other Accounts being hardly to be met with, or relied on) of three Sons of *Cham* (the fourth being believed to have been *Childless*) we find two of them were seated in *Asia*; only *Mizraim*, for the Name, shall
be

be allowed *Egypt* ; part whereof, *viz.* on the other side *Nilus*, must be in *Afia* too ; that *River* being the bounds to thefe two fpacious Quarters of the World. It being alfo not to be forgotten, that the *Philiftines* (living alfo in *Afia*), were his Off-fpring : Nor will this concerning *Mizraim* (for we have nothing but the concurrence of the *Name* to prove it) bring any great comfort to the Caufe, if we confider its Remotenefs from the parts we fpeak of, and the many great changes (probably (if known) no lefs objectable againft the reft) thefe *Egyptians*, or *Mizraimites*, fince firft carried Captives by *Nebuchadnezzar*, that is, for above two thoufand Years, have felt. In fo much that the true *Egyptians* do feem fince to have been fwallowed up, and even loft in thefe Conquefts. And now fuppofing the like of the other parts of *Africa*, from which no *Region* in the World can boaft of an Exemption, what certainty or ground can there be for *Conjectures* of this nature?

9. But to come nearer to the Matter: Either the Sons of *Noah*, with their Families, kept themfelves *diftinct*, each of them united in a body by it felf, or elfe did intermingle and live together, without regard of fuch diftinction of Tribe, or Family. If the firft, then 'tis evident that the Family, or Tribe of *Cham*, following *Nimrod*, its Head, did feat themfelves in *Shinar*, and the parts adjacent, unto which the holy Scripture gives witnefs. But if the fecond, then what certainty can there be from whom any Nation or People is derived, the *Jews* only excepted? Now it is plainly recorded by *Mofes*, *Gen.* 10. that *Nimrod* the Son of *Cufh*, *Cham*'s Nephew, *began his Kingdom at Babel*, in the Land of *Shinar*, (for that caufe, *Micah* 5. 6. called *the Land of Nimrod*) and from thence went and built *Nineveh* in *Affyria*, far enough from *Africa* ; which, if *Jofephus* fpeaks truth,

was

was left for *Epher*, *Abraham*'s Nephew by *Keturah*, and his Children, to be by them poffeffed, a long while after; and *thefe* no Defcendents from *Cham*, but from *Shem*, his Elder Brother.

10. But left thefe Tranfactions of *Nimrod* might be pretended to have been after he had travelled into *Africa*, and left a Colony there; (to omit the tedioufnefs and difficulty of the way) it is faid exprefly, that they journyed thither from the *Eaft*, not to be underftood of *Africa*, which is *South* from thence. 'Tis true indeed, the Scripture fpeaks of the *Earths being divided in the days of Peleg*, but determines not what that *Divifion* was, whether of its Inhabitants *Minds* and *Affections*, or that which happened upon the Confufion of Tongues; or whether it were about this or that way of *Worfhip*, and of *Religion*. Or even fuppofing it to have been no lefs then a parting, or dividing the feveral Territories and Quarters of the World; yet, unto which of their Lots each Parcel or Province fell, who had *Africa*, or which went to *America*, we there meet with no Account, or at beft but a very *dark* one. And for that of *Jofephus*, as it labours with the like uncertainty, fo it is not for their purpofe to *mention*, for the *Reafons* there given.

11. And whereas the learned Dr. *Heylen* fuppofeth this Quarter of the World to be Peopled from *Arabia*, by *Cham*'s Pofterity, croffing the Red Sea: He fhould in the firft place have fhewed how fo great a part of *that Family* diverted another way, not to be imagined if the Tribes each of them kept together. And then, fecondly, Why this might not be as well done by any other of *Noah*'s Children, confidering the *improbability* thereof, upon the account of the other Journeys and Aboads made by *Cham*'s Pofterity. And fo much for the firft Suppofure.

12. THEIR

12. THEIR second carries a more apparent Falsity, *viz.* That, that severe *Imprecation* of *Noah*, was denounced against *the whole Family of* Cham; whereas 'tis evident that none besides *Canaan* his youngest Son, was *mentioned*, and therefore not concerned therein; it being no less than thrice, *Gen. 9.* expresly said, that *Canaan should be their Servant.* And so before, *Cursed be Canaan, a Servant of Servants shall he be.* Now whatsoever may be presumed of the nearer Inhabitants of *Africa*, (which also is disputable) there is not the least probability from *holy Scripture* (but certainly very much to the contrary) that the Remoter are *Canaan's Off-spring*, whatever might be suggested for his three Brothers. Now it ought here to be taken notice of, that in all *severe sentences found in holy Scripture*, we are not to strain the words beyond their *natural sense* And seeing *Canaan* alone was mentioned, (for which reason his Children are, *Wisd.* 12. 11. stiled the *accursed Seed*) there remains not any likelihood for our *Negro's* being concerned therein. For 'twas in *Asia* that the *Canaanites* dwelt. There *Abraham* sojourned amongst them; and there *Joshua* afterwards found them. Whom having well near exterminated, he condemned the Survivers to be *hewers of Wood, and drawers of Water to the House of God*, Josh. 9. 21. & 23. 27. Which sentence was afterwards by *Solomon* confirmed, and more fully executed, 1 *Chron.* 2. 17. So that in the whole, this supposed *Imprecation* of the *Patriarch*, doth seem to be little more than a *Prophecy* of the *Canaanites* overthrow and reduction, under the Power of the *Israelites, Shem*'s Posterity, some eight hundred Years after to be accomplished; but not plainly an absolute Curse, or determination thereto. Even as the recording thereof by *Moses*, doth seem to have been especially done only for *Israel*'s justification in *dispossessing* of them.

13. But

13. But our *Negro's* who are quartered in the Remoteft parts of *Africa*, may juftly be concluded as too far diftant from *Paleftine*, to be any way concerned with thefe *Canaanites*; whofe *guilt* was no doubt then *expiated* by their expulfion and lofs of their *Country*, and of their *Liberty*, together with the *deftruction* of fuch who did abide the brunt of the War, or were detained afterwards.

14. However, fuppofing *Servitude* to be the thing intended in that *Imprecation*, (or *Prediction*, as I rather believe it) and that our *Negro's*, improbable as it is, were the very *Parties* concerned therein; yet, as it toucheth not their *Right to Religion*, (which I fhall immediately fhow, fo) neither doth it therefore confer any *Right* or Authority over them upon any, nor *commiffion us* to be the Executioners of the Sentence: Any more then *Jeremiah's* threatning of *Jerufalem*, did juftifie *Nebuchadnezzar's* burning it, and murthering the Inhabitants; for which *he was to expect a fearful judgment*, Ifa. 10. & Jer. 25. *&c.* And fo *Ifaac's* fore-fight and prophetic Declaration of *Efau's* fate, *Gen.* 27. and the fall of his Pofterity under his Brother's power, did confer on the *Ifraelites* no Right of thus Tyrannizing and Domineering over their *Elder Brother's* Off-fpring; as will appear from *Deut.* **2.8.** compared with the forementioned place in *Genefis.* Befides this Sentence upon *Canaan*, being once fo *thorowly* executed, there is no reafon it fhould now again be *repeated*, even fuppofing that (for which there is no ground), the *Negro's* are his Iffue; it feeming too *unmerciful* to punifh Men to that extremity twice, for one and the *fame* Crime.

15. THEIR third *Suppofition* is the continuation of this Punifhment, which our People are defirous to extend to the laft Man of that Generation, againft whom 'twas firft denounced; notwithftanding no
mention

mention is made of any beyond *Canaan's* Person.
Now this, as it is contrary to that so equitable a *Rule*
in expounding of Scripture, which I before mention'd ; so it thwarts the *Method* which God Almighty
useth in punishing *Offenders* ; who seldom or never
stretcheth the *iniquity of the Parents*, beyond *the third
and fourth Generation*, where the *Children* do not add
new Guilt of their own. And thence it is that we
reade, that these very *Canaanites* we are speaking of,
notwithstanding the *Curse*, whom, of all other, it was
most likely to reach, had their punishment deferred *till
their own Sins* had more fully deserved it, as may be
seen, *Gen:* 1 5.16. And therefore the unjust effusion of
the *Gibeonites* Blood was, 2 *Sam.* 21. revenged upon
Saul and his bloody House ; tho in truth they were no
other than the *Off-spring* of these *cursed Canaanites.*
Besides, God hath been pleased since to declare, that
*for the future, there should be no more occasion to use that
so harsh and ill relishing Proverb in* Israel, *of the Father's
eating of sower Grapes, and the Childrens Teeth being set
on edge :* For *that from thenceforth the Son should not
bear the iniquity of the Father, but that every Man should
suffer for his own Sins,* Ezek. 4. 20. & 18. 2. And
even in the Curse of *Eli's* House, 1 *Sam.* 2. That
*they should die in the flower of their Age, and that there
should not be an Old Man of his House for ever :* Yet
upon their Repentance, and a betaking themselves to
a sedulous study of the *Law*, 'tis said by one, that the
Curse was turn'd into a *Blessing*, and the line *Masculine*,
before always dying *young*, lived to an *honourable Age.*
" For God, saith the same Person, changeth his pur-
" pose concerning the punishment of Men upon their
" Repentance. And as [*for ever*] doth in the *Hebrew* Idiom , appear many times to intend no more
than some *considerable* space of time, which yet by God's
Mercy may be shortned ; so had that Particle been

E.

here

here affixed to *Canaan's Curse*, which it is not; yet there is no question but (as the Apostle testifies of the obstinate *Jews*) that *they also may be grafted in, if they abide not in unbelief* and impenitence; *for God is able to graft them in.*

16. THEIR fourth *Supposure* is borrowed from the fancied *nature* and *design* of this *Curse*; which some will affirm to be a kind of *Transubstantiating* of them into Beasts; others, to strike not only their *Souls* (in this Life), but to be an irrecoverable devoting them to Perdition and Misery *in the Life to come.* Whereas the *Text* mentions no more but Servitude in the *Curse*; not to be exceeded in the *Gloss*, or Interpretation, where the words are void of *Ambiguity*, especially in *severe* Cases. And this Service was also restrained to his *Brethren*, which cannot be supposed to be spoken of the *Devils*; it was to touch only their Bodies; it being not in the least probable, that *Righteous Noah* would curse the Soul of his Son, which was *none of his*, had he been so uncharitable; but was derived from a better *Author*, and therefore beyond his power: God having declared, that *each Soul is his; the Soul of the Son, as well as of the Father*, Ezek. 18. *And out of whose Hands none shall be able to pluck them*, St. John 10. And then as to the other part of these pretended effects; Should we suppose our *Negro's* to be the very Seed of *Cham*, and that they were no less under the Curse: Nay further, that that Curse had been denounced against the whole Posterity of that *graceless* and *unhappy Son*; yet as we have no assurance of the first, so neither doth it follow that *Servitude* should be attended with such *dismal effects*, as of Men to transform them into *Brutes.*

17. Which objected *Brutality*, had it carried any appearance, or likelihood of truth, could never possibly have escaped the notice of (at least) the wiser *Jews*

and

and *Heathen*: Who for the general, are found to treat'
them with a contrary *respect*. For the *Jews*, I
shall instance only in the *Septuagint Interpreters*,
who, as it is to be observed from *Psal.*74. 15. & 87. 4.
did none of them scruple to allow their Ἀιθίοπες (the
general currant Appellative both in *Greek* and *Latine*,
(like as *Cush*, the name given to *Chani*'s Nephew,
Nimrods Progenitor, is in the *Hebrew*) for those footy
People, the *Negro's* of those times) the ftile of Men.
To these I might also add St. *Luke*, *Acts* 8. 27. but
that possibly it may be replied, that he was none;
wherefore I shall let that pass. But for the Heathen,
Lucan in his *Pharsalia*, *lib. 9.* brings them in as Partners with the *Arabians* and *Indians*, in the worship
of their God *Amon*, who it seems had *monopolized*
him to themselves; for so much the *Poets* words do
seem to imply

> *Æthiopum quamvis populis, Arabumq; beatis*
> *Gentibus, atq; Indis unus sit Jupiter Amon*, &c.

And long before him *Homer*, in his *i Il.* bespeaks
Jupiter and his fellow *Dieties*, as vouchsafing them
their presence at a Banquet, and to become their
Guests,

> Ζεὺς γὰ ἐπ᾽ ὠκεανὸν μετ᾽ ἀμύμονας Ἀιθιοπῆας
> Χθιζὸς ἤβη μετὰ δαῖτα: θεοὶ δ᾽ ἅμα πάντες ἕποντο.

He in the same place conferring on them the character
of [*unblamable,*] as is to be there seen; nothing of
which had been compatible, nor any way suited with
the quality of *Beasts*. And to shew that those differed
nothing from *ours*, their *Complexion* is prov'd to be black,
both from the *sacred Writ*, as *Jer.* 14. 25. and from
the same *Poets* and Writers of the Heathen, particu-

larly

larly from *Ovid, l. 2. Met.* where speaking of *Phaeton's* burning of the World, he thus discants upon it, as to the *effects* 'twas believed it had upon these People;

> *Sanguine tum credunt in Corpora summa vocato,*
> *Æthiopum populos nigrum traxiffe colorem.*

And from *Juvenal* in his second *Satyr:*

> *Loripedem rectus derideat, Æthiopem albus.*

And likewise from his sixt,

> ———— *Effes*
> *Æthiopis fortaffe Pater : Mox decolor hæres*
> *Impleret tabulas, nunquam tibi mane videndus.*

And that they were a distinct People from the *Arabians* (contrary to what some have, I fear, without ground conjectured); Also, that they were seated from them *Westward*, at least nearer *Italy*, where *Lucan* wrote, than the other were; his method and order in muftering them, doth partly imply. And laftly, That the Scripture *Æthiopia*, (no lefs than this of the *Poets*, and of the other *Heathen*) was in *Africa*, lying between *Egypt* and the *Red* [or *Arabian*] *Sea*, and confequently the fame with ours, The Scripture doth in two places of *Ezekiel*, viz. Chap. 29. & 30. (in both which *Ethiopia* and *Egypt*, are reprefented as Neighbours, but the firft (agreeable to what was above mentioned) bearing the more diftant Situation ;) And alfo in the 68 *Pfalm* (where the fame things are obfervable, as in the former) doth not obfcurely intimate. And this I have added by way of prevention, and to defeat a little Argument of our Adverfaries, moft impertinently borrowed from the above mentioned groundlefs Conjecture of fome one

or

or two of our Writers, *viz.* That the Scripture *Æthi-*
opia (and even the Heathen too), was fituated not
in *Africa*, but in *Arabia*; That fo nothing there recorded, might be faid to concern our prefent *Negro's*,
nor be alledged in their favour.

18. Which yet, if certainly true , will not upon
Examination , be found fo advantagious to them :
The diftance of *Guinea*, our *Negro's* Country, being
confidered. For if the Scripture *Ethiopia* be in *Arabia*,
then, for ought appears, *Guinea* (and even the reft of
Africa) is clear of the *Curfe* ; fo that more is loft by
that Argument, than it ever got. Again, if according to the fignification of [*Cufh* and *Æthiops*,] they'l
allow its Inhabitants to have been *Black*, (not denied
by any hitherto, and it being no lefs confonant to
what is before faid thereof ;) 'twill make as much for
our *purpofe*, or even more. For thus it is ufually dif-
courfed ; Becaufe they are *Black*, therefore they are
Cham's Seed ; and for this under the *Curfe*, and therefore no longer *Men*, but a kind of *Brutes*. But contrary hereto, I fhall thus argue : Either all *Negro's*, or
black People, are of *Cham's* Race ; or fome are not :
If the laft, then 'tis evident there will be no neceffity
for our *Negro's* being under the Curfe ; But if the former, 'twill follow, that notwithftanding the *Curfe*,
they might, in the general opinion of the World,
ftill continue to be *Men*. To conclude ; I do not in
the whole, fee that this *Curfe* did touch any more than
the Perfons, Goods, and Poffeffions of *Canaan* and his
Pofterity ; who fome eight hundred Years after, were
to fall into the power of *Abraham's* Children : When,
the *Canaanites* being fubdued by the *Ifraelites*, and the
remainder of them condemned to Servitude, that prediction was accomplifhed to the full.

19. Their fift and laft Suppofition is borrowed from
the *horrible Decree*, (as one calls it) of *Reprobation*.

For

For tho our People are for the general no great friends to that *severe* Doctrine, as being too frightful for them to hear of, yet *in this case* it must serve the turn. But granting it true, that a certain number of Men, and amongst the rest this whole People of *Blacks*, and even all the rest of *Cham*'s Race, were thus devoted to Misery, and become the objects of God's Wrath ; yet will not this justifie our barring them of the Knowledg and Exercise of *Religion*. For they that hold this Doctrine, do nevertheless affirm it our duty, *To tender the Gospel unto all* ; And that, first, because they are uncertain who they are that are thus *Reprobated*, (and doubtless ours have had no new Revelation concerning it) : And, secondly, because their refusal (of which our *Negro*'s are not guilty, it having never been *tendered* to them) is to be a principal *Motive* for their Condemnation. So that nothing in this Doctrine, taking it altogether (tho we should suppose it most *Orthodox*) doth prejudice the *Negro*'s *Right* ; at least excuse our not tendring the *Gospel* (to omit food and bodily Necessaries) to them, whether in order to their *Salvation*, or further Damnation.

20. And thus these ridiculous Suppofures of themselves *vanishing*, as not able to endure a narrow Scrutiny or Examination ; it will not be amiss if, after all, we bestow some little time to enquire into *matter of Fact*, and consider the *Event* of things; ever held for the safest way of *interpreting* Prophesies. In searching into which we shall find the whole current of *History*, (so far as we have any certain Records, wherein mention is made concerning *Cham*, or his Posterity) to be no other than as it were a plain *refutation* of these groundless Fictions. For in the Bible, *Cham*'s Grandchild, *Nimrod*, is represented the first Monarch. And *Egypt* (or *Mizraim*) is described as a place of Learning, and its Inhabitants a free People, holding some of *Shem*'s Posterity in Bondage,

dage, for above two hundred years. And after their subjection to the *Chaldean* Yoke, not more Slaves than most other Nations in their feveral turns have been, and fome even to this day are.

21. And then for the *Abiffins*, fuppofing them *Cham*'s Race no lefs than our *Negro's* ; we have them reprefented in Hiftory for a very *flourifhing People* : As in a Treatife written originally in *Portuguez*, by one who had fpent many Years there, is to be feen ; which Treatife being fince tranflated into *Englifh*, was by the *Royal Society* ordered to be made public. It begins thus. " The *Abiffins* Emperor (vulgarly *Presbyter* " *John of India*) is Lord of the moft ancient and lar- " geft Dominions of thofe many Kingdoms and Pro- " vinces, into which *Africa* is divided. The Empire, " the moft Eafterly part of all *Africa*, called *Æthiopia* " above *Egypt*, &c. And then, *Pag.* 5. & 6. this Em- " pire anciently commanded many Kingdoms and Pro- " vinces ; their own *Annals* , and fome Hiftorians, " count above twenty, with almoft as many Provinces. " What at prefent paffeth for current is, That its " greatnefs *was once Notorious*, tho now limitted to five " Kingdoms, each of them about the bignefs of *Portugal* ; " and to fix Provinces, every one little different from " *Beyra;* or *Alenteyo*, two Provinces in the fame King- " dom. Thus much that Author. To this I may, tis poffible not impertinently, add that of *Memnon*, in *Virgils* 1. *Æn.* who is there ftiled *Niger*, but yet a free Prince ; who, with others from the *Eaft*,

(Eoafq; acies & Nigri Memnonis Arma.)

Brought his Forces to affift the *Trojans* ; and being, agreeable to his Name, by Authors reputed for a *Black* or *Negro*. The Queen of *Sheba* alfo in *Solomon*'s time, and *Candace* of *Æthiopia*, *Acts* 8. (if their Dominions

wer

were not the fame) were in all probability in their
feveral times great Princes, (as by the rich and fplen-
did Prefents of the former, with the great Officers
and Attendants of the others Court, (one of which,
being her *Treafurer*, was withal a *Dynaft*) is moft evident) : And yet by all Writers, are confeffed to have
ruled over Subjects naturally Black, being in all likelihood fuch themfelves. And their Kingdoms fuppofed by divers, to have been no other than that very
Æthiopia, above defcribed by our Author; to which,
he faith, *Their own Annals, and moft Hiftorians do
agree.*

22. So alfo as to their Incapacitie for *Religion*,
(A thing that never yet fell
under the Cognizance of the *
Gentiles (as the fore-mention-
ed Quotations out of *Lucan*
and *Homer* do witnefs), tho

** Nor yet of either Jews
or Chriftians before we very
luckily contrived & thought
upon it.*

poffibly that may be pretended as occafioned through
their want of our knowledg in the Scriptures:) by
virtue of this *Curfe*; the like *Events*, together with
the many *Prophetic* Difcourfes of the *Bible*, do no lefs
evidently befpeak the contrary. For *David* in the
Pfalms, we find doth mention them twice. In the
firft of which, *viz.* Pfal. 68. 31. *Junius* in his Notes,
affures us that the Prophet there fpeaks, *De amplitu-
dine Regni Chrifti*, of the large extent of *Chrift's* Kingdom, through their accefs thereto. And in *Pfal.*87.4.
amongft divers Names there recited, he fuppofeth that
David magnifies the Goodnefs of God for his purpofe,
of bringing all thefe feveral forts of People *into the
Church*. And then he immediately acknowledgeth
them for, *Cives ejufdem Ecclefiæ*; *Fellow Citizens with
the Saints, of the Houfhold of God*, and Members of
the fame Church with them. And in *Pfal.* 72. 9.
the *Eremicolæ*, there mentioned, who fhould come to
worfhip

worship *Christ*, are said by the *Septuagint Interpreters* (who 'tis possible might best be able to guess at the Nation pointed at in that Pariphrasis) to be no other than the *Æthiopians*, as in the said Translation may be seen. And *Acosta*, *l. 1. c. 4. De nat. nov. Orbis*, assures us, that the learned do hold, That the Wise Men who came to worship Christ, were as well of *Æthiopia*, as of *Arabia* and *Persia* : *And for this end*, saith the Almighty by *Zephania*, Chap. 3. 10. *will I turn to the Nations a pure Language*; *that they may all call upon the Name of the Lord, to serve him with one consent*: *Even from beyond the Rivers of* Æthiopia (not improbably pointing at the very South of *Africa*) *shall my suppliants bring mine Offering*: There being no *Curse* nor *Reprobation* of that force as to prevent their Conversion, *when heartily endeavoured*; or to make their Services at *God's Altar less acceptable* unto him.

23. Agreeable whereunto in a great measure (tho in a much *greater* it might be, did not the *God of the World rule so mightily* in some Mens Hearts) hath the issue of these Prophesies been, since the *Publication* of the *Gospel*: They being admitted into the *Church* almost as early as the *first Notice* of it. Both the *Egyptians* (amongst whom St. *Mark* was Bishop), and the *Ethiopians*, unto whom St. *Matthew* and other of the *Apostles* preached, *being in Christ* (St. *Paul's* Kindreds high Honour, as himself, *Rom. 16. 7. glorieth*) *long before our selves*. And the Holy Ghost especially commanding St. *Philip* to preach to the *Eunuch*, a Nobleman (as is supposed) of the same Country. By whose Zeal and Authority, the work was doubtless much promoted. For otherwise it would scarce have been there perfected so soon, as we find it was; and withal *so settled*, as not to be unfixed ever since. They even to this Day retaining their Christianity; if at least the Scripture *Æthiopia* be the same with that in *Africa*,

Africa on the Red Sea, which themselves do affirm, and some places in the Bible before recited (numb. 17 of this Section) do not obscurely declare. But be they the same or not, 'tis certain those are Christians, whom we speak of; and have so been for a long time; as (besides the former *Author*) *Alvarez* (a *Portugal* also) doth in his *Historia Æthiopica, l. 1. P. 171.* testifie. So also the *Author* of the *Atlas Major, P. 3. 52.* in *Æthiopia*; and *Le-Blanch,* a *Frenchman*; and *Sands,* one of our own Nation, in his *Journals :* Not to omit the Testimony *Viva voce,* of one of their own Bishops *Zabo-Zago,* an Ambassadour thence into *Europe.* To which may be added the Kingdom of *Moni-Congo,* in *Africa,* some two Centuries since Converted by the *Portugals,* which our own Histories do mention. And then for those pieces of *Africa ,* that were either part of, or conterminous upon the *Roman* Seigniory, and whose Shores were washed by the *Mediterranean* Sea; we find in the second and third Centuries, several hundreds of *Bishops* governing the Church there: Of whose number, tho at different seasons, were St. *Cyprian* Arch-Bishop of *Carthage,* and St. *Augustine* of *Hippo,* two the most Pious, Learned, and Eminent Fathers of their Times, or since. And even the Kingdom of *Nubia,* situated in the more inland Parts, were once Christians; tho now, *through the want of Preachers,* degenerated into their former *Heathenism,* or else *poysoned* with *Mahumetan* Impostures: Which is a consideration of so sad a nature, that we ought to make no further use of it, than to curb our own Presumption, and to bless God that it is not altogether our case, (*tho I must confess the distance from it is not great*): Our unthankfulness having long since deserved such another total Excision. And that as Heresies have ruin'd *Africa* and *Greece,* so Faction and *Atheism,* being with us no less prevalent, must needs in a short time, over-

grow

grow the true Branches in the natural *Tree*, so as to consume the spring of true *Christianity*, and suck out the juice of right *Religion*, leaving to us the Bark and Rine only, to be called *Christians*. *He that spared not them*, will find as little reason to pity us.

24. But to return from this Deviation. If in the last place we look unto the *Gibeonites*, *the true Posterity of Canaan*, and the most certain Issue of *Cham :* These (as they are supposed to have been those *Nethenims*, so often mentioned in *Ezra*, and *Nehemiah*) so it is evident that they pertained to the service of the *Temple :* Which, had this *Curse*, or their persisting in their former *Gentilism*, stood in the way, could not have been allowed. And in our Blessed *Saviour's* time, one of the same Stock, *a Woman of Canaan*, as St. *Matthew* terms her ; a *Syro-Phœnician*, a *Greek* or *Gentile*, as St. *Mark* bespeaks her ; both of them, *A dweller upon the Coast of Tyre and Sidon*, (now *Canaan begat Zidon*, saith *Moses*, *Gen.* 10. 25. and so in the 1 of *Chron.* 1. 15. and *Deut.* 1. 7. the Territory thereabout is said to have been the Patrimony of his Children) hath this *Eulogium* given her from his Divine Mouth, that her Faith was great ; whereby, tho thrice rejected *for a Dog*, yet she still persevering, did by her Faith and Importunity, so prevail, as to accomplish her desires. To these I might also add, that this was the Country of the *Widow of Serepta, or Zerepha, a Town belonging to Zidon*, 1 Kings 17. 9. (and by *Obadiah*, ver. 20. expresly declared to be *the Canaanites Possession* ;) unto which Widow, *Elijah* was sent ; tho there wanted not Widows in *Israel* at the same time, as our Saviour witnesseth, to sustain the *Prophet*, or that needed to have been sustained by him. And thus from the whole, these two things do appear most evident ; First, How not only uncertain, but rather, unlikely it is, that our *Negro's* should be *Canaan's* Off-spring. And, secondly,

condly, How derogatory it is both to *Reason* and *Religion*, that this Curse should touch either their Souls or Bodies, so as to deprive them of that *natural Right to necessary relief for both*, which is born with them, and *can never be separated from them.* Religion, especially the Christian, making no such *distinctions*, which our Sloth and Avarice have suggested to most of us. And if the Blessed *Jesus* did with so little patience, hear his Disciples urge to him a respect for his earthly *Relations*, surely much more must he have been incensed, had they proposed to him either *Stature* or *Countenance*, or any other the like *perishing Vanities*, to have become the objects of his Favour. Nor is our *Negro's blackness*, which gives the pretence for these Impieties, (in all probability) occasioned by any other means, than the *Climate* they live under. The remoter Inhabitants, within either of the more temperate *Zones*, (as upon the *Cape of good Hope*, and about *Fez*, and *Morocco*) being of a brown Complexion, answering to other swarthy People, in our *cooler* Regions. And whereas 'tis objected that here in *America* under the same Degrees, the like Blackness is not found in the Natives; It is to be answered, that neither is there the same heat, by them to be endured; our *cooler Breezes* (which *Africa* wants) being here the constant attendants upon the *Sun's* motion, and with him for the most part gradually *Rising* and *Falling* throughout the Year, in all the Regions of *America*, lying under the *Torrid Zone*. But to determine the whole matter in a few words : Since this Argument against the *Negro's* is drawn from holy Scripture, (no other Ancient Author mentioning either the Crime or Punishment, nor for ought we know, so much as the Name of *Cham*;) there is no reason why those Persons, who in all other of their Discourses, do *scoff* and *flout* at it, should be allowed even those just and lawful

ful Advantages derivable from that Scripture, which they in other cases seem no more to believe, than they do the Alcoran: And which they mention but with the same respect with the scriblings of our giddy *Enthusiasts*; but with far less, than they allow most other, even the *prophanest* Authors.

§. III. 1. And thus having finished the *First*, I come to the *Second* Objection, by which they hope to evacuate the *Negro's* Right to Religion: which is pretended to be forfeited, *If not by the Curse, yet without doubt by Slavery.* Religion being (forsooth) a kind of *Spiritual Gentility*, which with them must be lost or forfeited, by putting on the *Iron Chain* of Bondage. For certainly no less can be collected from those customary Replies and Demands, usually returned upon any Advices for the Christianizing of their *Negro's*, viz. *What, such as they? What, those black Dogs be made Christians? What, shall they be like us?* With abundance more such like Questions. And here I cannot but observe, that as this latter is extendible to all Slaves, of what Complexion or Nation soever, and no less to *Englishmen* and *Christians*, than to others; so the former doth intrench upon as considerable a number of *Mankind*, even a third part of the World; and that without all respect to their *Condition*, as in the other; Both Freemen and Slaves being there equally involved in the *same* Calamity, as in this, *Christians* and *Heathens* are; thereby as it were damming at one blow, two thirds of the World; all which, or more, do fall under one of *these* Capacities.

2. And so (after taking notice of their *Zeal* in being thus ready to take the advantage of such *Forfeitures*) having examined the first, I come to the second Objection: Wherein I cannot but see enough at the very first *view*, to move pity and commiseration
towards

towards these People, the *Negro's*, and that even more than when they were reprefented as *Brutes*. Their Humanity here ftanding them in no further ftead, than to make them more *Miferable*, than as Brutes they could poffibly have been. For whereas a *Brute* may according to the Scripture (which is a Book of *Reafon* and of *Juftice* too) in fome fenfe have a *Right* to divers things, the Slave muft be *devefted* of all. For by *Mofes's* Law, *The Afs finking under his burden*, had a Right to be relieved by the next Traveller, *Exod.* 23.5. Nor was the *Ox* to be *muzzled which did tread out the Corn*, Deut. 25. 4. his labour meriting better Ufage. And one of the Reafons for the Sabbath reft was, *Exod.* 23. 14. *That the Ox and Afs might have re-fpite from Toil, as well as their Owners.* (We fee here, no working them to death was allowed.) And *Solomon* in effect pronounceth that Perfon *unjuft, who regards not the life of his Beaft*, Prov. 12. 10. So that here is a plain Right belonging unto Brutes, whilft by us it is denied unto Men, *whofe Flefh is as our own:* A thing greatly deferving *to be laid to Heart.*

3. For in truth the very Heathen were never fo void of *Bowels* and tendernefs to their Slaves, as to deny them a *due Right* to neceffaries for their Prefer-vation. To which purpofe it is, that we hear *Cicero* thus pleading in their behalf, *Off. l. 1. Meminerimus autem etiam adverfus infimos juftitiam effe fervandam. Eft autem infima conditio & fortuna fervorum; quibus non male præcipiunt, qui ita uti jubent ut mercenariis, ad operam exigendam & ad jufta præbenda.* That is, *We muft take notice that there is a Right belonging unto Slaves,* * † *whom they that advife us to treat as hired Servants, in exacting their Labour, but allowing them their D.U.E, do not advife amifs.*
Nor

* *That by* Servus *is meant a* Slave, *this in* Terence, (Ego poftquam te emi a parvulo, feci à fervo, ut effes libertus mihi) *doth plainly fhew ; befides, that I find this place fo rendred in* *a Translation made many Years since.* † *In which words we are to observe three things:* 1. *The difference between* Servus *and* Mercenarius. 2. *That there was in* Cicero's *opinion, a* Right *belonging to the first.* 3. *That, tho unrestrained, he thought it our duty to treat even those, whom he there esteems of the* lowest Rank and Condition of Men (*and that sure must be Slaves*) with Mercy.

Nor is *Phocilides* less kind and just unto them, if at least we will admit Θεράπων & δ͂ϗλος, to signifie that condition ; which this Injunction doth demonstrate.

Γαϛρὸς ὀφειλόμενον δασμὸν παρέχϗ θεράπϗσι :
Δϗλω τἀῦΙα νέμοις, &c.

That is, *Defraud* not thy Slave of his *D U E,* but allow him his full proportion of Diet, and other Necessaries. Which the ensuing Prohibition doth more fully explicate.

ΣτίγμαΙα μὴ γράᵱηs ἐπονειδίζων ΘεράπουΙα : ʹ

Therein giving us to understand, who, and what they were he designed this Kindness to ; such ignominious *Stigmatizings,* being not to be imposed on any besides *Slaves.*

4. And that no other than such (properly so taken) are there by our *Poet* to be understood, is I think no hard task to prove. Θεράπων, being by *Hesychius* explained by ὀικέτηs & δ͂ϗλος: Both importing the same with *Verna* and *Mancipium,* in *Latine* ; The first being, as I have shewed (*Pag.* 32.) by *Siracides,* put in opposition to ἐλεύθεϱος, a *Freeman.* And the second [δ͂ϗλος], both in the *Septuagint,* and New Testament, plainly implying the same condition. For *Psal.* 81. 6. the *Israelites* condition in *Egypt,* is called δϗλἡα : And in *Psal.* 105. it is said of *Joseph, That he was sold,* ἐis δ͂ϗλον, *for a Bond-servant,* as we have it rendred from the *Hebrew.* And *Heb.* 2. 15. we find

δϗλἡα

δυλία, translated *Bondage*. And, *Apoc.* 19. 18. we have ἐλεύθερος ἢ δῦλος, *Free* and *Bond*. Add to this the *Jews* tart and quick reply, St. *John* 8. 33. ὐδενὶ δεδυλεύχαμῳ πώπότε, to our Blessed Saviour, discoursing of *making them free*; thereby setting the verbal δυλέυω, in opposition to ἐλευθερόω; which Saint *Paul* also twice doth, *viz.* 1 *Cor.* 9. 19. & *Gal.* 2. 4. The last of which is interpreted, *A bringing into Bondage*. So χαῖαδυλόϊ, 1 *Cor.* 11. 20. As also that of the *Jews* before unto our Blessed Saviour, as in the place will further appear.

5. But because it may seem proper, and to some perchance prove more satisfactory, to *confront* one *Heathen* with another, and so to explain the meaning of each, (altho the *Greek*, both of the *Septuagint* and *New Testament*, be certainly no less *Authentic*): I shall therefore be bold to summon in one for an evidence in this behalf, unto whose Testimony they cannot refuse to yield; And that is the most eloquent Comedian *Aristophanes*, in his *Plutus*; At the very entrance into which, one (stiling himself by those two forementioned *Appellatives*) is heard to complain of his Master's *sottish and unreasonable Impositions*; which yet, he confesseth, *he could by no means avoid, because*, as he adds,

Τῦ σώματος ὐκ ἐᾶ τ κύριον
Κραῖεῖν ὁ Δαίμων, ἀλλὰ τ ἐωνημένον, &c.

Fortune had deprived him of the happiness of being at his own disposal, by placing him under the Purchasers power. And certainly, he can be neither Freeman nor Hireling, that is become the Purchase of another Man.

6. Nor let any one object, that the above-mentioned Writers, like *envious* People, destitute of *Slaves* themselves, were more partial in their Rules to others; few or none in those times being *without some*, whilst

divers

divers poffeffed *many*. *Plutarch* writes of *Lucullus*, that he had forty thoufand; and that by their labour he levelled fifteen Mountains. And the trouble to which the *Romans* were often put to fupprefs their *fervile* Infurrections, (whereby it may be feen, that *Slaves may rebel without Religion*, and *that Chriftianity is not wholly in the fault, if any fuch thing fhould happen*) doth fhew that that *free People* were no ftrangers to fuch *Domeftic* Utenfils, nor to the Profit accruing by them to their Owners. Nor could *Cicero* eafily have amaffed together fo great Wealth, to the which, he was never born, without the labour of *Slaves :* 'Tis certain, he retained fome in his Family, which his fetting one at liberty, for the *News* he brought of the *Senates* Adjournment, (whereby he had a Day more given to compleat his *Oration*) doth manifeft: Nor is it to be imagined, that he then parted with all he had. But the words [*Libertus & libertinus,*] fignifying a *freed Man*, and the *Son* of fuch a Perfon, and made to diftinguifh [*liber & ingenuus*] from one that was *manumiffed* ; that is, Perfons *originally* Free, from fuch as were but lately made fo ; do enough declare the no want of *Slaves*, even amongft thofe who thus affert their *Right*, and condemn all their *unmerciful* ufage of them.

7. But to proceed : Had Slaves no *Right* at all, all *Laws* and Injunctions againft *oppreffing* them had been unjuft, 'tis certain very needlefs ; for it had been no other than to infringe their *Owners Right* of exercifing his, it matters not whether Gentle or Cruel, Pleafure and Authority over them: which might be juftly practiced even to the utmoft extremity, were the Parties divefted of all *Right* to better ufage. Oppreffion being neither more nor lefs than an *over rigorous treating of thofe under our power*, beyond what juftly the one could pretend, or the other ought to *fubmit* to ; which in

F

this

this cafe could never happen. For what can he lay claim to, who hath nothing either *within* or *without* him, which he can call his *own?* Or what wrong is it to bar or deprive him of *that which is not his?* Thofe Laws therefore do confefs a *Right* in the Party, on whofe behalf they were made. Elfe that in *Exod.* 21. 27. *He fhall let his Servant go free for his Tooths fake,* had been impertinent and injurious. And *Job's* purgation of himfelf, *Job* 31. 13. *If I defpifed the caufe of my Man-fervant, or of my Maid-fervant, when they contended with me, &c.* had been idle and ridiculous, and an argument that he underftood not his own Privilege and *Right,* whilft he ftood fo nicely upon theirs. And no better had been the advice of *Siracides,* Eccluf. 7. 20, 21. & 33. 30, 31. ver. *Whereas thy Servant worketh truly, entreat him not evilly; nor the Hireling* (where note what the former were) *that beftoweth himfelf wholly for thee. Let thy Soul love a good Servant, and defraud him not of Liberty.* Again, *If thou haft a Servant, let him be unto thee as thy felf, becaufe thou haft bought him with a Price :* So that the *Servant* here alfo is a purchafed Bondman; whom yet we are to treat *as our felves;* and, in the next Verfe, *as a Brother.* The like alfo muft St. *Paul's* Exhortation (or rather Precept) to his *Coloffians* be, Chap. 6. 1. Mafters [παρέχετε] allow (not give) *your Servants* (for that agrees not fo well with what follows) *that which is juft and equal;* fuch things being not to be reckoned Gifts, which are our *due,* and to which we have a *juft Right.* So likewife to his *Ephefians,* Chap. 6. 9. *Where he exhorts both Mafters and Servants to Reciprocal Duties;* giving the former to underftand, *That the Mafter of them both* (fo the Margent tells us fome Copies have it) *was in Heaven; who* (in punifhing Injuftice in either Party) *would be Impartial.* Which, with many the like places, are to be underftood of

Slaves

Slaves purely fo taken, as may be proved from 1 *Cor.* 7. 21, 22. and from 1 *Tim.* 6. 1. Alfo from 1 St. *Pet.* 2. 18. in the firft of which, (omitting that out of *Si-racides*,) they are advifed to accept of *Freedom when offered*, being therefore at that time, no doubt, under Bondage ; as in the next *v.* they are plainly declared to *be under the Yoke.* Not to be underftood of thofe whom we ftile *Apprentices* (that is *Learners*) fuch being certain of Freedom, fo foon as it is convenient, or fafe for them. And therefore we have reafon to imagine that St. *Paul's* advice was given to Servants of an inferiour degree, and to whom Liberty might be more *fafe* and advantagious, even as it was more difficult to be obtained. Befides, he there chargeth every Man in general, *to abide in the fame Calling, wherein they were called*, that is, wherein Chriftianity found them ; unlefs (which is prefently excepted) they might *lawfully obtain their Liberty.* And the cruel ufage unto which, St. *Peter* intimates the Servants he wrote to were fubject, doth fufficiently manifeft, that their Condition was no better than direct Servitude, and that even to *Heathen* Mafters. For otherwife the Exhortation in his 1 *Ep. Ch.* 2. 18, 19, 20. and afterwards, had been improper ; fuch Rigour and Cruelty of *Chriftian* Mafters in thofe early and devout times, being unlikely to have efcaped his *Apoftolic* Cenfures and fevereft Menaces, if not to have coft the Authors a total rejection from the *Communion* of Chriftians. From hence alfo we may note, (no lefs than from Saint *Paul's* words, 1 *Tim.* 6. 2. *As many as have believing Mafters*) (which fhews that fome of them had not) ; that the very *Gentiles* then, were not fo ill natur'd and malicious againft Chriftianity, as to hinder their Slaves from *embracing it.* And throughout the Old Teftament, both *Abraham's* Servants, and the reft downwards, were no better than Slaves ; unlefs where we

find

find [*Mercenarii* , *Hirelings*,] for diftinction, added.
The word [*Slave*] being no where found in the holy
Scripture, except once by a mifinterpretation in the
Apocalyps. And the Latine word [*Servus*] taking
its derivation from [*Servatus*], and importing one
faved in Battel , by his mercy that took him : In
lieu whereof, by Cuftom, Gratitude and Neceffity,
he was obliged to do him Service the remainder of
his Life. So alfo in the *Apocrypha*, (befides that of
Ecclus.) *Raguel*'s giving half his Servants to his Son
in Law *Tobias*, *Tob.* 10. 10. And *Judith*'s fetting her
Maid free, *Judith* 16.23. And in the New Teftament,
St. *Paul*'s *Antithefis*, 1 *Cor.* 9. 19. and *Gal.* 2. 4. with
the *Jews* reply to our *Saviour*, St. *John* 8. 23. (all before mentioned) do plainly difcover the meaning of
the word Servant in holy Scripture, not to import a
Mercenary, or Hireling, but a meer Bondman, or
Slave. And fo from the whole may be collected,
That Servitude is no fuch forfeiture of *Right* , but
that a Slave hath as good a plea and juft claim to Neceffaries, both *for his Soul and Body*, as his Mafter hath
to his ftrength and *induftry* in thofe Works, about which
he is imployed.

8. No more doth that *Maxim* in the *Civil Law*, *That
whatfoever the Servant acquires, is properly derivable to
his Lord and Mafter, as the true and fole Proprietor of his
Servants Acquifitions*, interfere, or jar with this Right,
than any thing that hath been pretended befides : This
Right extending only to neceffaries for Life, not to fu-
perfluities or abundance, which are the things aimed at
in that *Maxim*. Thefe only, and not the other being to be
reckoned for Acquifitions, and therefore feizable to the
Mafter. Not but that there are fome that can fwal-
low this *Maxim* in its fulleft *Latitude*, and even extended to the Lives and Fortues of *Freemen*, whom (no
lefs than *Slaves*) they can without fcruple diveft of
all

all *Right*. Thefe fhall affure us, *That Men have no ftranger obligations to Juftice, than either Fifh, or wild Beafts, who prey upon, and devour each other.* And, *That God is no more honoured by* A. N. G. E. L. (wittily pronouncing the Letters thus feverally, with a fhort paufe between each) *than by* B. E. A. S. T. And therefore that fuch tendernefs and regard of Equity, is to be avoided as a great impediment to *Profit* ; *The only art or fcience to be ftudied, and applied by Mankind.* And no wonder that they who hold and practice fuch Principles concerning *Freemen*, fhould prove no lefs fierce fticklers againft *the Right of Slaves*.

9. But fuppofing that according to this *Maxim*, the Slave might *without fpot of Injuftice*, be by his Owner deprived of all *Right* to Temporal Priviledges and Provifions, yet can it never be admitted as to *Spiritual*, nor be extended to thofe Provifions which do concern the health and happinefs of their *Souls*, that is, *Religion*. But muft be underftood, and only confined to the *Goods* of this World: the Poffeffion and Enjoyment whereof may be fome prejudice, or abatement to others, that want them : which I am to fhew, can never happen in *Religion* ; and this I·fhall prove three ways.

10. *Firft*, From the confideration of the Nature of *Religion*, which being the Refult only of a *virtuous Mind*, and an *Act* of the *Intellect*, a thing purely *Immaterial* and *Spiritual*, cannot be fubject to the like inconveniencies with Bodies, compofed and made up of Matter. Nor is it to be *engroffed*, or made over ; but, as *Free-common*, is the true *Right* and Property of every Man. So that whilft other Goods may, and for the moft part are, poffeffed by a *few* ; and fome do want, whilft others do enjoy abundance ; *The goods of the Mind are fufficient for all* ; becaufe not limited, nor circumfcribed ; nor,'as the other, falling within .

the

the Meafures and Rules of quantity, whereby they become *Infinit.* And no Mans Acquifitions of this kind, are any *Diminution* to his *Neighbour.* Whence it comes that there can be no clamour nor outcry of Wrong or Injuftice ; and no Man can pretend this Enjoyment to be any leffening to himfelf by anothers fharing with him. A..d a Man may as well complain of his being robbed of the *Light*, or *Air*, becaufe his Neighbour refufeth to clofe his Eyes, or to retain his Breath ; as any Mafter can be fuppofed to feel an abatement of his either Subftance, or *Religion*, by his Slaves joyning with him in the fame *Divine* Exercife. *Religion* being the true *proprium in Commune*, where every Soul is at full *Liberty* (without any fear or danger of endammaging the refidue of Mankind), to affume as much, and as great a *proportion* thereof, as is needful for him, and as he can defire.

11. *Secondly*, This may be proved from the object of *Religion, G O D*; unto whom it wholly belongs, and whofe entire Property it is, as being the Creatures Tribute due unto him the *Creator.* Now certainly, *God* is not the lefs receptive of the Mafter's Devotion, for his being accompanied therein by his *Slave*, any more (yea, rather much lefs) than the *North Pole* can become lefs inftrumental to the Mariners fafety, and prefervation through the multitude of *Points*, at one and the fame inftant, directed to it. And there is fpace enough in his *Immenfnefs* and *Infinity*, for our fafe repofing, and his no lefs *fure* acceptance of the moft unlimited *affections* and praifes of innumerable *Souls*, confpiring therein at one and the fame time.

12. *Thirdly*, This may be proved from the *fubject* of *Religion*, the Soul of Man, which is only in *God's* difpofal, *Ezek.* 18. 4. And therefore cannot become the purchafe of *any* Mortal, tho the Cafe, or Body may ; but is entirely poffeffed by the Party, or Owner,

not-

notwithstanding his being reduced under Bondage. *There is no Man* (faith *Solomon*, Ecclef. 8. 8.) *that hath power over the spirit, to reftrain the spirit :* But the Soul can ftill exercife all her powers and faculties, tho in Chains, and in a Dungeon, or even like *Jonas* in the Belly of the Whale. *Where the Spirit of the Lord is, there is Liberty,* faith the Apoftle, 1 *Cor.* 3. 17. Even in the midft of Bondage our Thoughts are free, and a Man may think, and wifh, and pray, in defpite of his worft Enemies : And as our Bleffed Lord advifeth, we may *poffefs our Souls* under the hardeft Preffures and Sufferings. From which Confiderations, it will appear that the *Soul* of the Slave is no part of the *Mafter's* purchafe, nor can he by any means make it *fubject*. And therefore he hath no wrong done him (tho we fhould grant the aforefaid *Maxim*, to ftrike at the whole Temporal *Rights* and Enjoyments (which are but few) that a Bondman can pretend to) by his Slaves practice and exercife of Religion.

§. V. 1. Thefe Objections being *wafht* off, I come now pofitively to declare in the Affirmative, that a *Slave* both may be, and naturally is invefted with a *Right to the Exercife and Benefits accruing to the foul by Religion*; and that upon a threefold account, *viz.* Of *Creation, Divine Precept,* and of the *good and evil of Eternity*; to which laft, the Slave is no lefs fubject, and accordingly hath *equal hopes* with his Mafter to the other. Nor can any Mafter pretend to it upon other Reafons than thefe that are here laid down.

2. Now for the firft of thefe, *viz. Creation* ; this the Bondman hath in common with his Lord. That is, he is alike the Off-fpring of Humane Seed ; was alike fuftained in his Mother's Womb ; was born, and drew in the *common* Air, even as others do : *Nor is there any King that had other beginning or birth,* faith the Wife

Man.

Man. The like alſo is acknowledged by *Job*, *Did not he that made him in the Womb make me, and did not one faſhion us both in the Womb?* Job 31. 15. And as *all Men have but one entrance into Life, ſo they have the like going forth of it*, ſaith the ſame Wiſe Man, *Wiſd.* 7. And as the Slave was created *free*, ſo Death ſets him at Liberty, and reſtores him to the like *freedom* again. In the Grave both the ſmall and great reſt quietly together; For *there the Wicked ceaſe from troubling, the Priſoners hear not the voice of the Oppreſſor*; and even *the Servant is free from his Maſter*, Job 3. Now *Creation*, from which *Job* infers a Right due unto Slaves, is a tie of the ſtricteſt Nature, and ſtrongeſt Obligation of all other; becauſe unto it we are indebted for whatſoever we either have, or can pretend to. Conqueſt and Purchaſe (which do confer on the Lord his whole pretence of Right or Power over his Slave) being not poſſible to have been, had not this preceded. And even our Parents *Right* of Dominion over us, is infinitely ſhort of this; who in all that they contributed towards our being, were but *Agents* ſubſervient unto him, without whoſe Bleſſing no perfection could have followed. So that whatſoever we enjoy, primarily is from *God, our true Father*, and Creator. They being but Procreators, or Deputies unto this great Author of Life, and all things. Now this being *equally true*, both of Slave and Lord; and God *Almighty* having this original *Right* and property in every Man, which ſoveraign *Right* of his cannot by any after act of his Creatures be forfeited, ſo as to cauſe an *Alienation* thereof from him (for be the Poſſeſſion where it will, his firſt *Right* can ſuffer no prejudice): The Slaves Obligation and Right (I ſo call it, *it being a real Priviledg*) *to ſerve God*, continues firm and inviolable, and no leſs unalterable than his Lords. Nor can it be ſwallowed up, or loſt in any

new

new pretended claim, whilst that first Obligation continues the same, which originally it was. No prescription of time being of force against so *soveraign* a Power as that of Gods.

3. But secondly, Slaves have a *Right to serve God,* by virtue of his determinate Precept and Command for their so doing ; None of his *Laws* being limited to any certain *Order,* or *Degree* of Men ; but were given to every Man alike, *whether Bond, or Free.* For he that said, *Thou shalt not Swear, Kill, Steal, Lye, Covet, nor commit Adultery,* made no difference nor distinction in the direction of these Laws, either of *Lords* or *Peasants, Free or Bondmen.* But the Imposition being equally laid on all, must exact an equal tribute of Duty, from all. No *Dispensation* any where appearing for the omission of the *Duties,* either of *Morality,* or *Religion* to Potentates, any more than the tenuity or meanness of an *inferiour* Person, was ever in holy Scripture admitted as a tolerable excuse upon the like occasion. And this Impartiality, is more especially the *Credit* and *Ornament* of Christianity: which for that Reason is stiled the *Common Faith,* and the *Common Salvation;* St. *Jude* 3. and St. *Tit.* 3. Which as the *Baptist* preached, St. *Luke* 3. *All flesh should see;* that is, enjoy and partake of, if they had any liking thereto. And in pursuance hereof S. *Paul* at *Athens,* declareth, *That God had now commanded all Men every where to repent :* (words comprehensive and large ; and, methinks very appositely pointing to these so *late* discovered Regions: But to go on). For that as he writes to *Titus, The Grace of God which bringeth Salvation, hath appeared to all Men :* Such an Universality making it an Act of Grace indeed. And the same Apostle in his Preaching, warns all alike of *the Wrath of God,* revealed against all ἀσέβειαν ἡ ἀδικίαν, *Irreligion and Injustice of Men.* Both he and the rest in their

practice

practice, proving their Senfe to be as *unlimited* and unreftrained, as their words were general; fhewing themfelves in their *Epiftles*, no lefs exact and punctual in fetting *forth the Duty of Servants*, and *as careful for the faving of their fouls*, as for their Mafters. And being never fo befet with Bufinefs, (tho doubtlefs they had enough, as having the good of, not one fingle Diocefs or Parifh, but of the Univerfal, or Catholic Church, 2 *Cor.* 11. 28. in their thoughts and care:) fo as to neglect the Soul of the meaneft Bond-flave. Whom for their encouragement, he affures, that *God himfelf* did take efpecial cognizance *of their faithful fervices done unto Men*; who would not fail to recompence *whatfoever good thing any Man doth, whether he be Bond. or Free*, Ephef. 6. 8. And 'tis remarkable, that the preceding words to St. *Titus*, do in place immediately fucceed an Exhortation to Servants, thereby as it were pointing out the very Perfons to whom that Grace had been manifefted, *no lefs than to the refidue of Mankind*.

4. And to this agreeth the neceffity thereof: For *Vertue*, which is made moft effectual and operative by Religion, is alike requifite and commendable in all Men: At leaft if there be any difference, the *Credit* of it will redound moft to them, from it was *leaft* expected; that is, from Servants. But it is manifeft, how neceffary *Vertue* is, in that all Men do abhor to be unjuftly dealt with. And they that regard not *Vertue* themfelves, do yet expect it in their Vaffals. Whence fome are fo apt to applaud Integrity, and other good Qualities in their *Negro's*, and to blame and punifh the contrary. Nor can it be doubted but that good Qualities are as *requifite* in a Servant, as *Conjugal* loyalty is in a Married Perfon, or *obedience* in a Child. Now *Religion* is the ftrongeft exciter and fpur to thefe *Vertues*, *fixing* and *engraving* them upon

the

the Heart of Man, and making such deep impressions thereof upon the Soul, that the Party shall even *prefer Death to the foregoing of his Duty*; which heretofore hath been evidenced by innumerable Instances; some examples thereof have in this Age been produced. And then can any Man believe other, than that *Religion* is necessary for People of *this*, or of *any other* condition whatsoever? Or that it is not the Master's great *Interest* to have his Servants minds possessed, with principles of *true Piety?* The benefit whereof *is least to the Slave*, tho he gain *Heaven* thereby; whilst his Master (besides that, of which he is no less assured, by being instrumental thereto) doth in this World also reap *the desired fruit of his Servant's FIDELITY:* Which whosoever hinders, must therein be an *enemy* to that his own great Interest. In a word, God having sworn, *Isa.* 45. 23. (again repeated, *Rom.* 14. 11.) *That every Knee should bow to him, and every Tongue give him thanks, and glorifie him*; (unto which Service he hath furnished Slaves with Abilities and Parts suitable;) and having withal by his express Commands, imposed on them alike necessity thereof, (unto which doubtless they are obliged to conform, every Man being bound to be as *Good* and Vertuous, as *God* doth require of him : I say, these Reasons considered,) the prohibiting and disabling them for this Service, is certainly a most palpable deprivation of their Right, which is the worst I shall say of it here, and at this time.

5. But then in the third place, this Right I am speaking of, is no less evident from the *good and evil of Eternity*; which the Master and Slave are, according to their Merits, each of them to enjoy, or suffer alike. For as the Precepts are general, so also are the Threats and Promises. As for instance: *He,* saith our Blessed Lord, *that believeth, and is baptized, shall be saved; but*

be

he that believeth not, shall be damned, St. Mat. 16. And the great Apostle St. *Paul* indefinitly pronounceth *Sin* to be the *Wages of Death* to all alike, *Rom.* 6. And in *Rom.* 2. he denounceth *tribulation and anguish to every soul of Man that doth evil.* So also the Prophet, *Ezek.* 10. 20. resolveth the matter, that *the soul that sinneth, it shall die.* But on the contrary, *He that believeth on the Son of Man, hath eternal Life, and shall not come into Condemnation,* faith St. John 15. 24. And faith St. *Paul, Whatsoever good thing any Man doth,* (speaking of Servants) *the same shall he receive of the Lord, whether he be Bond or Free,* Ephes. 6. 8. Further adding, *For with God there is no respect of Persons.* Now the Slave's Soul being as precious, and his danger and hopes equal with his Master s. a Right to the due and necessary means, either to prevent the one, or to obtain the other, cannot be denied him : Unless we will suppose, *That God should Damn so great a number of Men, for the abominable Lucre of a few greedy Epicures and Mammonists.* It being not to be denied, but that it is a thing highly unreasonable to tie any Man to an end, and at the same instance to bar him of the means requisite thereto; and withal, to condemn him to a perpetual Death, for omitting those *Duties* (if at least we may so term them), when he had no Right nor Liberty to perform them. Wherefore since that the *Ways of God are all equal,* 'tis to be concluded, that whatsoever *Penalties* he hath decreed for the breach of his Laws, must be because there first was a *Liberty,* at least, if not an *Ability,* given for the observance of them; with sufficient means allowed both to obtain the *good,* and to avoid the *evil,* consequent to the *keeping* or *neglect* thereof.

6. I shall conclude my whole Proposition with a few Lines, to this purpose, borrowed from a *Sermon* delivered on a *Christmas-Day* in this *Island*; For which I

am

am sure the Preacher (who, tho his Discourse was
to *White People*, did yet design it for the benefit *of the
Blacks and Tawneys*, of which our fierce *Quakers* Spirit (see *P. 4.*) was quite Ignorant ;) will not be
displeased.   The Text being taken out of St. *Luke* 2.
the latter part of the 10th *ver.* his Discourse thereupon
was to this effect.   " And that we may not too proud-
" ly insult upon these People [the *Negro's*,] and with
" the *Poet*, resolve against them, — *Quod nulla sub illa*
" *cura Jovis Terra est* : — *That they are wholly without*
" *the care of Heaven, and of God's Protection and Provi-*
dence : That like the *Mountains of Gilboa*, no Dews
" nor Showres of Grace were to fall upon those parched
" Fields ; or like the *barren Fig-tree*, they were smitten
" with a perpetual Curse ; we find them admitted in-
" to the *Church* upon the first dawning of the Gospel.
" And *Acts* 8. We reade the holy *Spirit* of God, to be
" no less than thrice, particularly concerned, and acting
" for the Salvation of the *Æthiopian* Treasurer.; a con-
" descention so extraordinary and rare, that few, ei-
" ther Men or Nations, can boast of the like. Where-
" fore if St. *Peter* could from one single Example, in-
" fer the Salvation of *all the Heathen*, Acts 15. what
" should hinder, but from this *Eunuch's* ready submis-
" sion and hearty acceptance of the Heavenly Do-
" ctrine, we also may infer the Calling and Conver-
" sion of all the *Negro's*.   And since that God, *who*
" *knoweth the Hearts*, bare him witness, and did put
" no difference between *him* and other *Gentiles* ; but
" *purified his Heart by Faith : Why tempt we God*, in
" detaining them in Bondage to Hell (no less than to
" our selves) for whom Christ died, and redeemed
" them from thence ? —And then proceeding to that
" Example of *Ebedmelech*, Jer. 38. 39. he thus con-
" cludes ; —Both which being considered, it is most evi-
" dent (to use St. *Peter's* words in his Discourse to
" *Cornelius* ;)

" *Cornelius* ;) *That, to them alfo, hath God granted re-*
" *pentance unto Life* ; that they have Souls to be faved
" no lefs than other People ; and an equal *Right* even
" with us, to the Merits of *Chrift.* Of which, if
" through our Neglect or Avarice, they be deprived,
" that Judgment which was denounced againft wicked
" *Ahab,* muft befal us, *Our life fhall go for their's :* The
" lofs of their Souls will be required at *our Hands,* to
" whom God hath given fo bleffed an opportunity of
" being inftrumental to their Salvation.

§. VI. 1. My two former *Propofitions* being finifh-
ed, I proceed now to the third ; wherein, as a moft
natural Inference, the Injuftice of withholding this
Right from our *Negro's,* was no lefs pofitively declared. A thing fo *clear,* that had I not heard and feen
the contrary, more than a thoufand times over, I
fhould have thought it *impoffible* once to be queftioned,
or denied. For what can be more *unjuft,* than to deny
any Man an apparent Right ? Efpecially a Right of
that confequence even abfolutely neceffary, and where-
on *Eternity* depends. If it be injurious to deprive a Man
of his Houfe, or Goods, the enjoyment whereof is
confined to the duration of but a few Years, (and
yet fuch an *Injury* it is, as but few can bear) ; It muft
certainly be no lefs, (rather a great deal more) op-
preffive to thruft him out of thofe *Eternal* Manfions, and
from his Heavenly *Father's* Houfe ; to fupplant him of
his Patrimony in the *Celeftial Canaan* ; and, as much as
in the Oppreffor lieth, to rob him of the *Grace* of God ?
An Injury of an endlefs permanency, and for which,
no place for amends nor *reparation* can be found ! A-
gain, if the reftraining of ordinary Neceffaries, as
Food, &c. be an unmerciful *Cruelty* and Injuftice to
the Parties, to whofe *Prefervation* they are neceffary
and *due* ; How much more *Barbarous* and *Inhumane*
muft

muft it be to withhold from them the exercife of *Re-ligion*, and the knowledg of *God*, equally needful for the prefervation of their *Souls?* And if Slaves have a Right to fo much of their Labour as may furnifh them with the *firft*, (which, it is proved, they have) certainly it will follow, that their Right is as great to the *latter*. If the *Negro's* Mafter be in his Sicknefs obliged to afford him fuch *Succour* and Relief as may, if poffible, prevent the *Anticipation* of his Diffolution (for otherwife he is a Murtherer, and amongft *more vertuous Chriftians*, would certainly be *Arraigned* for one) doubtlefs he is equally bound to *prevent* his Damnation. It being, as the Orator teftifies, againft common Equity and Morality, to poft-pone a *leffer* evil to a *greater*; to deftroy a *Man* to fave a *Horfe*; or in a Man to throw away the *Nobleft* and moft *Precious*, to fave the more *Dungbil* and *bafeft* part of him; efpecially when obliged *with equal care* to preferve the whole; or if to beftow any more on either, to prefer the *beft*, and that Eternity be allowed the preheminence. And this care, which carries its *reward* always with it, is but a moderate *Retribution* of the Servant's Labour, tho to him of *infinite* value.

2. And here may it not be demanded, Why the *Mafter* who thinks this care as to *Religion*, needlefs for his *Slave*, doth (as fome would have it believed of them) hold it needful for *himfelf?* Since the meaneft Slave hath a Soul of no lefs *value*, and to be preferved by the fame means, with his. Or how comes his Soul, being of but one and the fame *fubftance*, to have a better title to *Happinefs*, and the means of attaining it, than the others, fince that the holy Scripture, the *Charter* of happinefs to Mankind, informs us of no fuch difference? Where the Servant that believes, is by St. *Paul* dignified with this Privilege of being the

Lord's

* 'Απηλεύθερος.
See the Margent,
1 Cor. 7. 22.

Lords* *Freedman*, and thereby qualified with a full Liberty and Freedom, to partake of the Immunities of *Religion*, and to the exercise of whatsoever *Actions* shall be conducive to promote his interest in *Eternity*, and to attain to the Blessings and Joys of *Heaven*. And this, being so plainly there asserted; and the most certain and *Catholic* Faith of all Christians; no Man that professeth an Assent to these, can, without contradicting himself, gain-say it : Yea, a very *Infidel*, may, from this owned and avowed Principle of Christianity, pass *sentence* against him, acting so contrary thereto.

3. And questionless from our *Negro's* being Slaves to argue their no Right to *Religion*, is more Oppressive and Injurious, than that Force which first made them so : Because striking at their *Souls*, and subjecting them to *Hell*, as much (only for a longer time) as to their *Tormenters* here on Earth : And to have avoided which, it might have been wished, either that their *Creation* had failed, or not exceeded this fancied state and degree of *Brutes*. And this Injustice must upon all respects, be heightned by the consideration of those great *Ends* unto which all Momentany advantages ought to give way: Nor is it to be understood as terminating only in the Sufferings of the *wronged* Party, but directed and glancing at Him also, whose the Soul of each Man is; whether in a Bond, or *Freeman :* And *who* cannot be thought to *resent* a Fact, so at once Sacrilegious and Oppressive, less than an Earthly Prince doth the *Murthering* of a *Subject*, the *Author* whereof is deservedly made with his own, to wash out and silence the loud cry of his Neighbours, or *Fellow-subject's* Blood. And as a *Crime* of this nature marks the *Oppressor* with the blackest Guilt, so it cannot but render him Obnoxious to the *severest* Vengeance, that a

provoked

provoked and *just God* can inflict upon him, both Body and Soul; and *probably, no less in this Life,* than *certainly in the other.*

4. I confess, as to the Provision for their Bodies, they deny it not to be expedient, or fit to be allowed them : But this, not as their *Right,* or *Due,* but as conducive to the Masters Convenience and *Profit, The most operative and universally owned Principle of this Place,* and indeed of the whole *Plantations.* They consider it only in order to the enabling their People to undergo their *Labour,* without which themselves cannot get *Riches,* and great Estates; but nothing (so far as I could ever learn) for the Wretches *Health* and Preservation. And their both Discourse and most current Practice, do declare no less; in neither of which doth appear much *Tenderness.* Pity to Humanity being here reputed a *pusillanimous* weakness, and a very back friend to Interest. Whence their Houses are so plentifully stored with tormenting *Engines,* and Devices to execute their *Cruelty.* So that the *Satyrist s Poetic* Description of those famous *Tyrannies* then practised in *Rome,* the true resemblances of what were of old practiced in *Sicily,* comes short of the reality of this. For in the very letter of his words,

Præfectura Domus Siculâ non mitior Aulâ, Juv. S. 6.

They here outdoing those precedents of *Cruelty,* tho the most Notorious, that *History* hath delivered to Posterity; as being persuaded, *That a Slave can claim nothing as his Right, besides Stripes and Labour.*

5. And as they exceed those ancient Severities, so the *immodesty* of the Executioners, 'tis to be presumed, did come short of what has here been the wonder of the new and *less-seasoned* Adventurers, to hear related. It being sufficient in those times to chastize a

G

Bond-

Bond-woman, ——*Nudam humeros, nudiſq; mamillis :* *Bare to her ſhoulders and breſts only :* Whereas here, thoſe who before were quite Naked, *all but a little* of their *middle part,* have this alſo uncovered : The *Miſtreſs,* to the ſhame of her Sex, (as from an Eye-witneſs and preſent Spectator, hath been atteſted to me) not bluſhing to be preſent (an effect, 'tis poſſible, of their believing *Negro's* to be but *Brutes*) amongſt a crowd of Boys and Men, to witneſs the Execution, no leſs than to prevent *Compaſſion.* The Tormenter (always of the *ſex Maſculine*) to keep even pace with our *Satyriſts* words, no leſs then with her Immanity,

(Et cædit, donec laſſis cædentibus— :)

Seldom giving over before quite tired ; which if too ſoon, doth argue Sloth, and is apt to be interpreted a *Connivance* ; a *Crime* big enough to endanger his Place, and to deprive him of the honour and happineſs of being *Archi Maſtix* of the *Negro's* for ever after. Which certainly are *Inhumanities* of the wrankeſt kind, and no leſs needing to be reſtrained by ſome wholeſome and good *Law,* then were the like formerly exerciſed by the *Spaniards* upon the poor *Americans.* But from which by a *Bull* of *Charles* the Fitth, then King of *Spain,* and *Emperour,* they were moſt gracioully releaſed. For which theſe alſo do ſeem to cry with their utmoſt earneſtneſs unto the Government *at Home* ; not doubting but that in time they ſhall be heard.

6. Nor are they very conſtant to that firſt and ſo very *agreeable* Principle, of preſerving theſe poor Wretches for Labour (their only end in purchaſing of them,) by a due *proviſion* of Food (not likely to put them to any extraordinary expences, whilſt little better than what the *Hogs* do feed on, and is, to ſave time, generally planted by themſelves upon *Sundays*) :

And

And of *Cloathing*, for which a *Canvaſs Shirt* and *Drawers*, during the two or three rainy Months (which is all the *Winter* we have here) will ſuffice: And laſtly, by allowing them time of Reſt, and of reſpite from Labour for their *tired* Bodies. I ſay, they are very far from a conſtant acting according to that *Principle* ; unleſs where the benefit of preſerving, ſhall exceed the dammage they are like to ſuſtain, by ſuffering ſome few of them to be *Starved*, or otherwiſe to *Periſh*. That is, If three or four Hundred may be more advantageoufly maintained (for it being uncertain which of them will out-live the other, they muſt be at like *Charges* with each, if they would *ſave* them all) then *fifteen*, or *twenty* new ones be purchaſed, to fill up the *dead* rooms, (for ſo many, or more, are like to be wanting at the Years end, without ſuch *Proviſion* :) I ſay, then 'tis poſſible that they may fall to conſult their God, I N T E R E S T, and endeavour their *Preſervation*. Which kind of Conſiderations are not ſo frequent among the *Mightier*, as with the Middle and Meaner ſort ; who do uſually find it leſs convenient to *buy new*, than (having but a few) to *preſerve* their old *Negro's*. Whereby both their and the *White Servants* (the general name for *Europeans*) condition, is leſs miſerable under theſe, than under the *richer* ſort ; with whom the death of a good *Horſe*, and of a *Negro*, is of equal moment, and doth uſually extort from them the ſame expreſſions of Grief and *Sorrow* ; unleſs where the Horſe doth happen to be of the greater *Value*.

7. To this alſo I might add, as an effect of their *ſcant* allowance of Food to their Slaves, the many *Robberies* and *Thefts* committed by theſe ſtarved People upon the poorer *Engliſh*. Of which, if I ſhould affirm their owners to be the occaſion, by thus ſtarving of them, I think I ſhould not hit much either beſide, or

be

beyond the *Mark*. That they are not difpleafed at it, *if dexteroufly performed*, is the general belief and fenfe of the *Sufferers* : And this is faid to be the true meaning of that cuftomary reply, *Tufh, they can fhift*, to the Stewards and *Overfeers* requefts for a fupplie of the *Negro's* want of Provifion. Which fufpicion of their Connivance, is further augmented by the fmall *Redrefs* that is given, or made to the injured parties, upon their juft Complaints ; unlefs taking them in the *Act*, they there fhoot them dead ; which is all the remedy they can get : Whereby the *Ifland* is daily deferted by its Inhabitants. And this alfo is one of the chief Reafons, why Provifions are fo *dear* ; no live *Creature* being to be raifed, or *kept fecure*, but under Lock and Key.

8. I might here alfo add, that the *Pickaninnies*, or young *Negro*-Children, except only the hardieft, wanting a due attendance and care of them, do moft of them perifh in their *Infancy*. Their *Mothers* continual labour in the Field, not admitting a neceffary care or regard of them.

9. Nor are thefe Miferies the Fate only of the *Blacks*, but, in a proportionable meafure, of the *Englifh* and *White People* alfo, who generally *are better wrought than either fed or taught*. And for their *charity* to the Sick, tho brought even to Death's door, yet can they hardly obtain the leaft amendment in their *Diet*, tho never fo earneftly importuned ; their *Condition* and Countenances no lefs *pleading* for them. I confefs, I would not here be fuppofed to charge all alike, where (poffibly) divers are to be excepted, *tho to me unknown*. And thefe things have, beyond all difpute, wafted more *Englifh-Men*, (not to mention *Negro's*, and other *Nations*) than are at this Day to be found in all *America*. Who with better ufage, might have been of great ufe to the Peopling of thofe vaft defolate *Regions* :
And

And at the same time, contributed no small Reputation and Strength to their *Mother-Country.*

10. And to give one Instance for all, of this Unmercifulness; it was concerning *one of these,* and even a *Natural Subject* of one of his *Majesties* Kingdoms, tho not of *England*; and for an Accident wherein another deserved the whole blame, (were any at all due, which is questionable) that that *execrable* Speech mentioned before, *Page* 69. was uttered. But for which, *right or wrong,* the poor Man sustained an hundred Lashes, or more. Seven *Rods,* each bearing five Sprigs (which occasions their name) nothing inferiour to our *Willow,* being spent upon him: Whereby he was, to the astonishment of the Beholders, (some whereof (no less than the party himself) are to me very well known) many days after, seen, as it were but one general *Scab,* all over. The barbarous *Author* of it, in contempt of their *Exstacy* and Affrightment, then venting that blasphemous Expression: And withal adding, *That it was no less lawful for Men, than for the Fish, or wild Beasts, the greater and more powerful to worry and destroy the rest.* A Speech better becoming an *Out-law,* than a *Judg.* But from hence may be argued, that if their Servants *Bodies,* in the sustaining whereof their *Interest* so much consists, do meet with no more mercy, their *Souls* must expect much less; from such who believe *Religion* an impediment to their *Profit;* and with our King *John,* do think, *That a Stag may grow very fat, without ever hearing of Mass.* And that if these be so much neglected, it cannot be imagined that the other should once fall under their consideration. Nor is this the effect of *Sloth* only, or a thing accidental; but by design, and from a principle (next to their supposed *Brutality*) springing from the imaginary *inexpedience* thereof: The *ground* and *foundation* of those *foul* Positions,

G 3   which

which have miniſtred but too *juſt* occaſion for this
Diſcourſe. Which fancied *Inexpedience* is the thing
that falls in my way, next to be conſidered and treated of.

Ezek. 8. 13.

*And he ſaid alſo unto me, Turn thee yet again, and thou
ſhalt ſee greater Abominations, that they do.*

C H A P. II.

That the Profeſſion of Chriſtianity *abſolutely obliging to the promoting of it, no* Difficulties *nor*
Inconveniences, *how great ſoever, can excuſe
the Neglect, much leſs the* Hindering, *or Oppoſing of it; which is in effect no better than
a* Renunciation *of that Profeſſion.*

§. I. n. 1. NOthing then having hitherto appeared of ſufficient force, to invalidate
our *Negro's* natural Right to the Privileges of *Religion*,
nor to acquit their *Injuſtice*, who hitherto have with-
held them from, at leaſt not acquaint them with it;
I come now to enquire whether certain great perſonal
Inconveniencies thereupon, as is pretended, neceſſarily
enſuing to their *Owners*; the many *inſuperable Difficulties*, or laſtly, the *numerous Miſchiefs* thereby threat-
n'd to the *Public*, (if found true,) may not prove a
ſufficient Bar, and even juſtifie their Maſters refuſal,
at

at leaft forbearance, notwithftanding this *Right*, to admit them thereunto.

2. Before I reply unto which, I fhall crave leave to demand of them, What Nation, or *Sect* of Men, did ever till now hold it Inexpedient, or *not fit to perform what was Juft and Right?* Certainly, none befides *Thieves* and *Cut-throats*, (or the late *pretended* Saints) fuch whofe whole fubfiftence was by Violence and *Rapine*, and therefore have been proclaimed *Out-laws*, and reputed as *common* Enemies to Mankind: Fit *Tutors* for thofe that profefs themfelves *Difciples and Scholars of Chrift!* And yet even thefe, as *Cicero* obferveth, *l. 2. Off.* are *forced to conftitute Laws, unto which they conform themfelves.* And by an Inftance of two noto-rious *Banditi*, who *by an even fharing of their Purchafe, arrived to great Wealth*, he further confirms his Argu-ment, for the neceffity of Juftice: Which, he faith, *doth confift in Equity, by fupporting the Weak againft Op-preffors, and obferving an even indifferency, in the admini-ftration thereof*, both to high and low. And therefore he tells us, that for this end, *Leges funt inventæ, quæ cum omnibus unâ atque eâdem voce loquerentur: Laws were enacted, which fhould indifferently fpeak the fame fenfe and language to all conditions and degrees alike.*

3. And doubtlefs 'tis a thing agreable to Nature, to maintain *Right*. A principle plainly legible in the Practice, becaufe firft planted and riveted in the Hearts, of the moft barbarous *Nations*. None of thefe owning other, but that what *was Juft and Right*, was alike *due to, and from all Men*; and then certainly to Slaves from their Superiours, fo far as that Right fhould extend. And this without any byaffing Con-fiderations by particular *Interefts*, but guided by *Equi-ty*, the moft exact Rule of *Right* and *Juftice*. Thefe being not *empty Names*, but importing *real Duties*; of which we are not to take our Meafures by the *vaft-*

G 4

nefs

ness of our *Ambition*, or our unbounded *Avarice*, but by the truest *Reason*, void of all disturbance by *Passion* and *Corruption* from by-Ends.

4. To prove which, I might amass together whole Pages of *Quotations*, out of the forementioned little Volumn of *Moral Duties*, but shall at present content my self with Gleaning only a few out of that full Stack, or Sheaff. As, *That the foundations of Justice are to hurt no Body, but to consult the Good of all. That we are born to Honesty, and that Justice only can confer on Men the Title of* [*Good.*] *That whatsoever is True, Simple, and Sincere, is most agreeable to Man's Nature. That nothing Cruel is profitable. That the endeavouring after Wealth and Estates by just ways, is commendable ; but the contrary base and detestable. That they do pervert the foundations of Nature, who do separate Profit and Honesty* ; It being horrid to imagin, *that any profit can be made by Injustice* ; yea, *even at that very time* when we *obtain* the thing *reputed thus profitable,* it being impossible that *these should conduce to any Mans benefit. That* Socrates *was wont to curse those Men, who first separated Profit and Honesty : Nothing being profitable or expedient, but so far as it is void of Baseness.* And most fully to manifest and evince this *Position,* is the whole work and design of that *excellent* Treatise.

5. And now let those *Christians* who pretend a Necessity, for that which *Heathens* have in their several Ages and Times, so fiercely declaimed against, *As misbecoming Men, and Unnatural* ; and do pretend a *necessity* for that which *no temptation of Profit* could induce them to accept, or assent to ; and further do hold it *convenient*, and even *commendable*, (as being the first step to *Honour* and *Authority* ;) to compass Estates by the most Sordid ways, which either the Examples of a *Corrupt Age*, or their own *fruitful* Inventions can suggest. And for this *false* end do deny their Slaves the

exercise

exercise and benefit of *Religion*, upon the pretended *Inconveniencies* and imaginary *Inexpedience* of it ; I fay, let them coolly weigh this *virtuous Heathens* refolutions *concerning the neceffity of Juftice*, and the *turpitude of the contrary* Vice ; and having fo done, let them bethink themfelves how little Right they have to that nobleft *Appellative* of *Chriftians* (if they at all care for it), who do thus profeffedly turn their Backs to common *Equity* and *Juftice*. And then to confider whether of the two, *Themfelves*, or their *Slaves*, by them kept in ignorance of their *Duty*, be the *blackeft* and wrankeft *Heathens*.

§. II. 1. And thus having from the confent of Nature and Reafon made it evident, that *Right* and *Equity* are in defpite of all *Inconveniencies* to be complied with, I fhall without further delay, betake my felf to my Affertion, before laid down, *viz. That the Profeffion of Chriftianity*, &c. Which will beft be proved by looking into, and difplaying to each view, the true Nature and Notion of *Chriftianity*, which I underftand to be, *A devoting of our felves to the Service of Chrift, and a ftrict Obligation in defiance of the whole World, to promote his Intereft and Honour, even with the lofs of whatfoever is precious or dear unto us*. Which Vow is to be fincerely and truly made and kept ; the whole Action being otherwife but meer *Pageantry*, and *Hypocrify*.

2. And that this is the true *Notion* and fence of *Chriftianity*, not only the exprefs words of that folemn *Covenant*, made betwixt God and our Souls, at our initiation into it by *Baptifm*, doth fhew ; but alfo our Bleffed Lord's fo often reiterated, and no lefs plain Declaration, in *Anfwer* to this very *Queftion*, do moft fully prove. As, when he forewarns his *Apoftles*, that *Self-denial* , and *a renouncing of Worldly Affections*, with a firm refolution to *undergo the Crofs*, that is,

All Losses and Sufferings, are Qualifications highly neceffary for all his Followers. He further alfo acquaints us, that *Houfes* and *Lands*, *Kindred* and *neareft Relations*, and even *Life it felf*, are all to be flighted as bafe and vile, in refpect of our Duty to himfelf; The very fubftance of our Vow in *Baptifm*.

3. And to place my *Affertion* beyond all Difpute, I fhall here further note, That this in all Ages of *Chriftianity* hath been fo underftood, even till this very Day. Hence St. *Peter*'s Profeffion, to *lay down his Life for his Mafter*, was accepted by him ; which he afterwards performed, as alfo did the reft of the Apoftles. And the holy Scripture inftances in St. *Stephen*, and St. *James*, both early *Martyrs* and Witneffes of this Truth. And had this been otherwife the Churches *Kalander*, had not fo long fince been furnifhed with fo compleat and numerous an Army of thofe Noble *Martyrs*, as to Mufter up five thoufand for *each day* throughout the Year. Who all of them, doubtlefs, might have faved their Lives, had it not been more for their Lord's *Honour*, and the *Intereft* of his *Religion* (which they were thereby to promore), thus to fuffer the *effufion of their Blood* for him, who by his own Example of *pouring out his Soul unto Death*, did firft lead them the way thereto. And in the *Hebrews* we have the examples of the Jewifh Martyrs, who were fawn afunder, *&c.* fet before us for our imitation, by St. *Paul* : whofe Afflictions alfo, muftered up in his latter Epiftle to the *Corinthians*, c. 11. with his frequent Exhortations to the like, and a *refiftance even unto Blood*, that is, in contempt of Death ; and of following *Chrift's* Example, of *fuffering for the Truth* ; affuring us that there is no other Way, or Gate, by which we fhould obtain an entrance into the *Kingdom of Heaven*, but *through much Tribulation*, Acts 14. do fufficiently evidence, that this Doctrine was not to

expire

expire with its great *Author*, but alway to remain a neceſſary condition of *Admittance* into his Service and Fellowſhip, ſo long as he was to have a *Church* upon Earth; that is, till the *Conſummation* of the World. Now, doubtleſs none of theſe were ſo much in love with Death, but that willingly they would have redeemed their *Lives*, at the loſs only of their *Eſtates*, or at leaſt, the whole with ſome part; could it have been done without offending their Duty. So that here were *inconveniencies with a witneſs*; yet there was no avoiding them, ſo long as they knew themſelves under this *Obligation* to their *Saviour* and Maſter *Chriſt*.

4. Now here ſome (I do not ſay all), will grant that they are indeed tied, *not to deny Chriſt*: But, ſay they again, are they therefore bound to proclaim him, or to perſuade others, who think themſelves *much better* (or as well) already, to become his Servants and Followers?

5. To which, I anſwer, That, I ſuppoſe, they are: And that, Firſt, as being *abſolutely bound thereto*, by their very *Profeſſion*; that is, *by their owning themſelves for Chriſtians*. The contrary being no leſs than a renouncing of it: Becauſe it proceeds from a neglect and even contempt thereof, than which nothing can be more contrary thereto. And which when not occaſioned through Fear, or by Accident, but ariſing from Choice and Election; and withal attended with a perſiſtance in and defence of it, is ſuch a clear indication of our diſaffection and no eſteem thereof, as to amount to a plain denial; which every ſingle Sin, tho of the groſſeſt kind, abſtracted from thoſe, doth not. And therefore no Chriſtian can ever juſtifie his omiting any poſſible lawful means for the advancement of his Religion; much leſs that which is indeed the Principal. Beſides, Chriſtianity is of its ſelf *a profeſſion*

of

of doing Good, and *of aſſerting* (not concealing) *the Truth*; which was the very end of our Bleſſed Lord's *coming into the World*; as himſelf, St. *John* 18. 37. witneſſeth, namely, *to bear witneſs to the Truth*; and *to ſeek and to ſave that which* was periſhing, or quite *loſt.* And therefore he was perpetually either imploying himſelf in preaching and *working of Miracles*, or going from Place to Place, and fetching many tedious and weary Circuits, to find out Patients to exerciſe his *Power* and *Virtue* upon, and to *Heal* their Diſtempers: Removing Mens *Diſeaſes* from their Bodies, thereby to work *greater Cures* upon their Souls: And, without partiality or diſtinction, curing *Servants* and *Beggars* of their *Infirmities*, reſtoring the *Blind, Lame, Deaf*, and *Dumb*, without any reſpect to the *quality*, but to the *need* of the Parties; and no leſs out of pure humanity and pity to the *Diſtreſſed*, than for the *ſatisfaction* of doing Good. And from this Example and Doctrine of the Bleſſed *Jeſus*, the firſt Chriſtians did not grudge to ſell their *Houſes* and *Lands* for the Relief of others. Nor were they to confine and determin their *Charity* to the bounds of their own Profeſſion (tho the *Houſhold of Faith* was in the firſt place to be ſupplied) but were obliged *to do good unto all Men*, not forgetting their very *Enemies*; much leſs their *Domeſtics* and *Slaves*, by whoſe Labour they had their whole Subſiſtance. Now if they thought themſelves obliged to relieve Mens *Bodies*, the worſer part, much more were their *Souls* to have a ſhare in this Charity: By their extraordinary *Care* for which laſt, and their *contempt* of the Miſeries and Sufferings of the other, when called to it, it was evident what value they did put upon each. As knowing that if *they gained the whole World, with the loſs of their Souls*, they ſhould have had but little left to be boaſted of. And if they held it their Duty to leave themſelves deſtitute

even

even of an *Houfe* for fhelter, and to part with their *Treafures* (the getting whereof did coft them fo much Sweat and Care) for the good of the *Church*, and the increafe of *Religion*, themfelves in the mean while depending only upon *Providence*; there is no doubt but they prefumed it much more their Duty to beftow their *Breath* and *Words*, which could coft them no Labour, befides that of *uttering them*; nor any *Expences* more than of the *time* therein laid out and imployed.

6. And conformable hereto, hath been the Practice and Confent of *Chriftianity* in all Ages fince. For firft of all St. *Peter*, being, *Acts* 4. forbidden *to fpeak any more in the Name of Chrift*, remembring his Commiffion and Calling, and knowing what a prejudice to the Souls of Men his filence would prove, He, encouraged from *Heaven*, with the hazard of his Life, perfifts and goes on, boldly in the moft public place (even in the *Temple*) like a true Minifter and Apoftle, *fpeaking all the words pertaining to this Life*, that is, to *Chriftianity*. And thofe Chriftians that *were fcattered abroad upon the Perfecution which arofe about* Stephen, travelled into remoter Regions; but *there preached the Word*; fome *to the Jews only*, whilft others preached to the *Gentiles* alfo : Both concurring in this Sentence, That they underftood it to be their Duty to promote the Doctrine of their *Lord*, in whatfoever Territory they fhould happen to be caft. This was the caufe of St. *Paul's* toylfome Journeys into *Syria*, *Greece*, *Spain*, *Rome*, &c. Others of the Apoftles piercing into *India*, and in a few Years fubduing more Kingdoms to *Chrift*, than the *Roman Eagles* had conquered in many Ages: Nor did Religious Chriftians think it any Difparagement to imploy their utmoft *Skill* to advance this Service. Befides, the Charity and Love of Souls, did heighten their *Zeal* to the effectual *deftroying the works*

of

of the Devil, and to rescue out of *his Snares, those that were taken Captive at his will.* Nor could they be at rest till they had established him, their most Natural Lord, in his *Hereditary* Dominions *over the Heathen,* and extended his Authority *even to the utmost parts of the Earth:* Such was the deep sense they had of this Duty. And therefore Tradition hath delivered, that the Apostles by Lot, like so many great *Generals* going to take in Cities, and conquer Provinces, forted themselves to travel into the most distant Regions, for the effectual carrying on of *this* great *Work:* Notwithstanding that *they knew there were no Dignities nor Preferments to be any where expected, besides Affliction and Martyrdom.* Whereof St. *Bartholomew* is said to have betook himself to *India* ; St. *Thomas* to *Parthia* ; St. *Andrew* to *Scythia* ; St. *Matthew* to *Æthiopia* ; and St. *Matthias* is said to have adventured amongst the *Canibals.* So that no *People,* how Barbarous, or Remote soever ; nor any *Clime,* tho portending nothing but Destruction and *Calamity* to them, nor even the most apparent and affrighting Dangers, could by any means divert them (as by an Instance we have, *Acts* 21. 13. of St. *Paul's* resolution, is manifest) from prosecuting *this so glorious a Design,* so much by us slighted : Who instead of taking such difficult Voyages, do (even the best of us) scarcely *wish well to them;* and do think it enough to propagate the Gospel in *Fable only,* and as at the *Isle of Pines.* Never taking care to teach the *Natives,* where we come, any *Good* ; but to learn them in all the *Evil* , which we practice our selves.

7. Nor did this Zeal die with the *Apostles,* and their immediate *Successours,* but did shine most brightly in the Christians of the following Ages : Neither *Sex* (according to its Capacity) believing it self *exempted from this Service.* For as Women are said to have been *Apostles* to the Apostles, so the *Iberians,* as *Socrates* delivers,

livers, *l. 1. c.* 15, 16. do own their firſt knowledg of the *Goſpel* to a *poor She-Captive.* Which no doubt was by her at firſt undertaken and aċted, out of a *ſenſe* of her Duty, (ſuch an opportunity being providentially adminiſtred to her); and the common Principles of all Chriſtians direċting her thereto.

8. After the like manner we read, that the middle *India* was converted by two Strangers, their Names *Frumentius*, and *Ædeſius.* And *Euſebius*, in his *l. 5. c.* 20. of *Eccl. Hiſtory*, writes of St. *Pantenus*, (whom he ſtiles *a moſt famous Man, for*) *that he ſhewed ſo much, and ſuch Divine Zeal for the Word of God, that he went to preach it to the Indians :* Either to ſubdue ſome new *Province*, or to perfeċt what another had begun.

9. And it was very early that St. *Peter*, or St. *Paul*, or St. *Simon Zelotes*, or St. *Joſeph of Arimathea*, or St. *Ariſtobulus*, or ſome other of the *Apoſtolic* Age (whoſoever they were) came into *Britain*, to give it the *Honour* of having *the firſt Chriſtian King.* And the *Britains* when invaded by the *Saxons*, did not, ſome of them (as St. *Kentigern*, and others) ceaſe to follow thoſe Examples ; they thinking it their *Duty* to do this *Service* to their very Enemies, and to preach to them, for their Salvation, who ſought their Lives, and their Countries Deſtruċtion. Tho this, being not ſo heartily carried on and purſued by them as was neceſſary, did afterwards give *Gildas* their Country-man, great occaſion of complaint againſt them.

10. For a ſupply whereof, St. *Gregory*, Biſhop of *Rome*, moved (as *V. Bede* piouſly diſcourſeth) *by Inſpiration from God*, ſent *Auguſtine* with other Religious Men to preach to the *Engliſh.* Who, being *converted to the Faith*, did themſelves become no leſs zealous *Propagators* thereof, both at home and abroad : Having been the happy Converters of the *Haſſians, Franconians,*

conians, *Turingians*, the *Saxons* of *Weſtphalia*, the *Friſians*, the *Hollanders*, *Norwegians*, and *Lithuanians*. For not to reckon up *Felix*, *Berinus*, and *Agilbertus*, St. *Aidanus* and *Columbanus*; all Foraigners, yet inſtrumental to the *Saxons* Converſion: Nor yet that Religious King St. *Oſwald*, who himſelf out of his great Zeal to promote the Faith of Chriſt in his own Kingdom, did not think ſcorn to become Interpreter to *Aidanus* as he preached, and to give the ſence of the Sermon to his Attendants, as *Aidanus*, who underſtood not *Engliſh*, delivered it. I ſay, not much to inſiſt upon theſs, we reade of St. *Willibrood*, *Boniface*, and Pope *Adrian* the Fourth, with divers other *Engliſhmen*, the Converters of theſe Nations; And our *V. Bede* tells us of the two *Henwalds*, ſuffering *Martyrdom* by adventuring into *Saxony*, upon the like Errand.

11. And ſo far were our Anceſtors perſuaded of the neceſſity of this Duty, that *if any thing happened amiſs to them, they concluded it to ariſe from this Neglect.* Hence *Kenwalchus*, King of the *Weſt Saxons*, obſerving his Affairs not to ſucceed very proſperouſly; he reſolves to amend that Fault: Of which Reformation he ſoon found the effects, in the Proſperity which thereupon enſued. *But all ſuch Conſiderations are ridiculous amongſt Atheiſts.* And therefore when one Mr. *A. B.* in *Virginia*, offered his Service in order thereto, he was laughed to Scorn by the *&c.* They, at leaſt ſome of them, with a Scoff replying, That thoſe who go upon that Work, are to *provide neither Purſe nor Scrip*; becauſe he had made ſome Propoſal alſo concerning Maintenance.

12. 'Tis true indeed, our *Church* upon the laſt *review* of the *Liturgie*, doth ſeem to have had an Eye thereto, when in Her Preface ſhe declared, "That the "*Office for Baptizing thoſe of riper Years, may be alſo uſe-* "*ful*

"*ful for the baptizing of Natives in the Plantations, and*
"*others Converted to the Faith.* Such was her tender
care for the Souls of the *Heathen,* in that most wholesome Provision. But, alas! the Enemies of Goodness have frustrated and defeated our hopes, so far,
that for any use the said *Office* hath been put to here,
it might almost as well have been left out. However,
from these few Instances which I have taken out of
Church History, as Water out of a common River,
(whereof every Man may take enough, without Offence or Injury to any other), may be seen how zealous former Ages were for the *Conversion* of Heathens;
which they looked upon as a Duty consequent to their
Baptism, and without which they could not challenge
the Name of *Christians.* And so much for my first
Reason.

13. But secondly, If this be not the Duty of Christians, then must *Christianity* fall short of the Piety of
Gentilism, whose *Philosophers* and Learned Men, as they
aimed at nothing so much as the knowledg and *dis-
quisition* of the *Truth;* so next of all was their desire of
converting and winning others, with them to embrace the same. Who yet knew nothing of any Reward thereof, beyond the *satisfaction of doing Good,*
and of being instrumental to advance *Society.* Which
Considerations ought to be more prevalent with *Christians,* as having promises of *Rewards for whatsoever
good thing* is done by them, *not only in this Life, but in
that which is to come.* And the Heathens Notion of a
Good Man, was from hence derived, *viz. From doing
all the good he could:* Whilst they held a self-ended Person in the greatest detestation. Now Christianity is
but *Morality,* strained to the highest pin : And therefore our Lord prescribes to his Disciples, the *righteousness
of the Scribes and Pharisees,* (that is, of the strictest
Jews) not only for our bare Imitation, *but to be out-*

H   *done*

done by us. One of whose *principal Vertues*, we reade; it was that they *compassed Sea and Land to make Proselytes.* And certainly then a Christian is much more obliged thereto.

14. Thirdly, We are hereunto tied by our Covenant in *Baptism* ; wherein we promise *to fight manfully against Sin,* which no man can fully answer, that doth not first fight against *Infidelity.* Hereby also we engage to be faithful Servants to *Christ,* during the Term of our whole Lives : Which work of Converting Sinners, is the most *grateful* service that we can perform. For certainly it had otherwise never been so often prest and recommended with such promises in holy Scripture ; As, *He that winneth Souls is wise,* Prov. 11. 30. *And they that be Wise, shall shine as the Firmament, and they that turn many unto Righteousness, as the Stars for ever and ever,* Dan. 12. And *the reducing one fallen from* (and surely 'tis the same if he never knew) *the Truth,* is in some sense made *Meritorious,* St. *James* 5. 20. Nay further, it is so much our Duty, that 'tis Heathenish to neglect it, as (besides what I have before in this *Sect.* said) may be inferred from those general words of the 4th *Chap.* and the last *Ver.* of the same *Epistle.* And if by the Husbands causless Repudiating of his Wife, he in that Act *causeth her to commit* (and so is guilty of her) *Adultery* ; by the like parity of Reason, *He that hinders his Servant from believing, must be guilty of his Infidelity.* And in a word, so natural it is for Men to promote the Faith which themselves do believe, that with the Barbarians of *Japan,* we may safely conclude them for no *Christians,* that do neglect it. And not only as in our subjection to Earthly Masters, to whom our Strength and Labour is due ; but in this Covenant of Baptism, we bind and make over our Souls and Affections to *Christ,* no less than our Bodies. Now let these be but *Cordially*

dially imployed by us, and 'tis not possible but they must reflect some *improvement* to this Service. Especially where the Agent is fully armed with *absolute* Authority, and those on whom he is to lay out his endeavours being his *Slaves*; and so, tho *disaffected* thereto (which they are not)yet might soon be brought over, by one having *Power* to make them submit and bend their Inclinations to his *own*. Tho at first perchance less cordially (that is, where there is any dislike, which I must avow that here there is not ;) yet in an outward Compliance at least; And even this disaffection, *custom* and long *use* would in time *wear out*, and make the contrary become *Natural*.

15. And this doth seem to come down to our Case, wherein we have a perfect concurrence in all the parts, except only *in the Principal* The *Masters* professing themselves *Christians*, their Slaves being indeed *Infidels*, but giving no proof of any Malice, or disaffection to *Religion*. The *Masters* armed with full power over them ; and having themselves *vowed* to imploy that whole Power, and *all that is theirs besides*, in the Service of *Christ*. Yet for a petty inconsiderable *Interest*, to be certainly recompenced with much greater Advantages (as will soon be shewed), *refusing to promote that Faith* (which they themselves do own) *among those of their own Families*. Now if this be to comply with such *Obligations*, then may it be concluded, that a Christian hath a mighty Advantage above other Men ; and that he may, without the least *guilt* or *stain* to his Soul, both *swear and forswear* whatsoever his *Interest* shall persuade him to.

16. I confess, I do not hold it to be alike every Man's Duty to labour herein ; but do yet dare to affirm it every *Christians* Duty to concern himself about it, so far as his condition of Subsistence and living, and his *knowledg* shall enable him. For as Mr. *Glanvil*

in his *Dialogue concerning Preaching*, P. 57. tells us,
" Every private Chriſtian may, and ought to preach
" in this Senſe. Every ſuch is a *Prieſt* to his own Fa-
" mily ; that is, it is his Duty to teach them the great
" things of *Religion*, according to the beſt of his Skill
" and Knowledg. This is one way to *provide for our*
" *Families*, and 'tis the moſt neceſſary. *Men had better*
" *neglect the getting their Children and Servants Bread and*
" *Clothes, then to omit their care about this greater and*
" *more needful Proviſion.* It's true, 'tis not perchance
every Mans Duty to traverſe the World from one
Quarter to the other, to preach the Goſpel, and to
Convert *Heathens.* But if they happen to be brought
Home to us, and made members of our Families, we
are, *beyond diſpute*, each Soul of us obliged, *as we ten-*
der our own Salvation, to endeavour theirs. That Interrogatory, 1 *Cor.* 7. 16. *How knoweſt thou, &c ?* carrying in it an Argument greatly enforcing the like *cha-*
ritable care and endeavours for the ſaving of *others*,
tho lodged at a remoter diſtance from us, than our Boſoms :
For he whoſe whole buſineſs it is *to do good*, muſt never be *idle*, whilſt there are any objects of his Charity,
eſpecially under his Roof : For he fails of his *Duty* ſo
much, as he falls ſhort in any particular *Office within*
his power, though of an inferiour nature to this. And
if unmercifulneſs be the only Crime obſervable from
our *Saviour's* Charge at the Day of Judgment, repreſented, St. *Mat.* 25. Doubtleſs, they that have thus
cruelly treated their *Slaves* ; and, what in them lieth,
deſtroyed their Souls, ſhall then find an *Hell* hotter than
ordinary, and like *Nebuchadnezzar's* Furnace, *heated*
ſeven times more ; and a *Devil*, proportionably mercileſs,
provided for them. Where they ſhall come (too late) to
know, that *God doth above all things deteſt Hypocrites*,
and that he *will by no means endure to be yoaked with*
Mammon.

§. IIII.

§. IIII. 1. But here forgetting the *absolute* necessity of this *Duty*, our People to acquit themselves, do offer some things by way of *Excuse*: As, 1. The *Difficultie*, and, as they pretend, even *Impossibility* of effecting any thing upon them. 2. Their want of *English*. 3. Their *Stupidity*, and utter *incapacity* for Instruction. Lastly, Their *irreconcileable averseness* and hatred to all *Religion*. All which are certainly *false of the major part of them*, at least of *divers*, as my self, upon my particular knowledg and experience can truly affirm. But as to the second, there are, 1. Many who have lived a considerable time in the *Island*. 2. Others that were born in it. A 3*d* sort that have been brought up and baptized in *England*; who can *all of them speak English*, no worse than the natural born Subjects of that Kingdom. These I presume will make more than one *moity* of the whole. And for the rest, even the very *Novices* of them, I do not see why they should not be as capable of *Religion* as of *Business*. But it is notoriously known, that even those of the *third* sort (when Trapand hither) are as little regarded as the rawest *Barbarian* in the whole herd : And so of those whom themselves have caused to be Baptized in *England*, whereof I have spoken, *P.* 37. in the former Chapter. And it is no less certain, that their very *Domestics*, that attend them in their *Chambers*, and at their *Tables* (the rest living in sheds, and separated places *without Doors*, purposely allotted for them) are taught to avoid the room (which also *hath been observed of them in* England) as often as Prayers do happen to be said or read : As if there were some secret Charm, or power of doing mischief in Prayers. Nor are they forced thence out of any *scruple*, or (superstitious) fear *of having their Services polluted, by the intermixture of Unbelievers* (a Nicety never here heard

H 3   of)

of); but only upon this Suppofition, of *the no neceffity thereof, nor benefit to Negro's, or other Slaves.*

2. And as for their *Averfenefs*, a charge moft proper to be returned upon the *Objecters own Heads*; I
have always found them rather *fond and defirous* of being made *Chriftians*, than any way *averfe* thereto;
which a certain paffage in Mr. *Ligon's* Defcription of
this Ifland, will further evince: Tho, as in that cafe
(and *here I will fuggeft the worft*), this defire might poffibly firft arife only from an Ambition of being like the
Englifh : Which fhould be no wonder, efpecially in
People, who have never fo much as heard *whether there
were any Salvation, or Heaven for them,* but rather the
contrary. But our People being extraordinary Wife,
have to prevent further Trouble, always taken it for
granted that their *Negro's* have an Antipathy againft
Chriftianity. Nor are they upon a due trial and experiment *defirous to underftand other.*

3. And here, if it might not occafion too great an
expence of Time, (for which reafon I fhall be brief)
I fhould crave leave to rehearfe a Portion more, of the
above mentioned *Chriftmas* Difcourfe, wherein I have
an *Apologie* for them upon this Account, ready formed
to my hand, in thefe words: —"But are their Inclina-
"tions fo much altered from what they were? Surely,
" the facred *Text* doth furnifh us with too notable Ex-
"amples of Piety and Goodnefs, in thefe People. The
" firft is that of *Ebedmeleck,* Jer. 28. whofe compaffi-
" on to that *Prophet* in interceding for him, and there-
" by delivering him out of the *Dungeon,* was fo highly
" pleafing unto God, that in the next Chapter we find
" this high commendation and *Eulogium* given him,
" *That he had put his truft in the Lord* ; and therefore
" had a promife of prefervation from thofe *fatal* Cala-
" mities, which fuddenly befel that *ftubborn* People, a-
" mongft who he then lived.

4. " The

4. " The fecond is that of Queen *Candace's* Treafurer, *Acts* 8. who though a *Dynaft*, of great Au-
" thority with his Prince, travelled fo long a Journey,
" only to worfhip God at *Jerufalem*. Judg all the
" World, whether this *African*, notwithftanding the
" *blacknefs of his Face*, had not a *whiter Soul*, than
" moft of our *European* refined Chriftians ! But this is
" not all ; behold him fparing no time from his Devo-
" tions, but, *As he fate in his Chariot, he read the Pro-*
" *phet* Ifaiah. And then fee him attentively liften-
" ing to the Heavenly Doctrine of St. *Philip*, earneftly
" thirfting after the Baptifmal Waters; Which having
" obtained, he *goes on rejoycing*, and hafting to make
" known *the glad tidings of his Saviour* to his Coun-
" try-men. It was this *Noble-man's* commendation,
" that he did not think himfelf too great *to be God's*
" *Servant*, and that *amidft his Pomp, he could attend*
" *Religion :* And to give him his due praife, I do not
" fee but that this *black Prince* may be a Copy for the
" beft of us to write after ; a Pattern *worthy the bright-*
" *eft Profeffor's Imitation* ; and of whom, to ufe our
" Saviour's words, I may fay, *Verily, I have not found*
" *fo great Faith, no not in* Ifrael, &c. By which words
of this *Sermon*, the Preacher doth evidently confute
this malicious fuggeftion, touching the *Negro's* pretended natural averfion to *Religion*. And in truth,
fome of our People do in part confefs no lefs, when
in *England*, to prevent *Obloquy* (not regarded by o-
thers of them) for the Credit of their Ifland, (and no
lefs to make a fair fhew) they procure, at leaft give
way to, the *Baptizing* of their Attendants, as I have
before mentioned. (Like thofe in *England*, who to
fave their Places and Credits at once, do dare to be
guilty of that fuperftition at twenty miles diftance,
which they will not adventure upon nearer Home).
It were to be wifhed upon their return, that, laying

afide

aſide that ſuſpicion of *Averſeneſs*, (which they there-by grant to be but a *Fiction*), they would remember to compleat *here*, what they *there* began. It being to be preſumed that the many thouſands remaining, have *the like precious Souls* , tho not bleſſed with ſetting foot upon *Engliſh* Soil. But this would go near too much to affront the Principle here, (of which, Mr. *Ligon*, whom I but now mentioned, gives an Account in the Reply that one made to him, upon a Motion of the like nature) and *ſcandalize* their *weak Brethren* : Who might be apt to ſuſpect them for *Chriſtians indeed*, and *Apoſtates* to the Cauſe; ſhould they openly perſiſt to commit a thing ſo contradictory *to their long continued Irreligion*.

5. Howbeit notwithſtanding theſe ſo *pregnant* Inſtances, and their own knowledg and experience to the contrary, to make out this *Averſeneſs*, they relate a ſtory of a thing called a *Chappel* belonging to a private Family, wherein a *Preachment* (for *Sermon* I ſhall not call it, the *Speaker* wanting his *Orders*, together with divers other very requiſite Qualifications) was made each *Sunday* in the Afternoon ; the *Holder-forth* (notwithſtanding his ſaid *Infirmity* as to *Orders*, &c.) being uſually taken up in a *Parochial* charge in the Morning. Now unto this our ſtupid *Africans*, being admitted, (for which *Supererrogation*, the good Man *the Maſter was heartily laught at*, tho without cauſe, as I ſhall ſhew :)

With this Perſon it was cuſtomary for him to Bap-tize in the Neighbouring Pariſhes ; and that at under-rates (which was e-nough to ſpoil the Trade.) He would alſo joyn Couples in Marriage, and do any Offices where Money was to be got : the Miniſters being not able to prevent nor hinder him ; The Veſteries (*who* are our Supreme Church-Governours) *not favouring their Complaints, as being themſelves not willing to be confin'd : Nor have the* Mi-niſters, *even* thoſe in Orders, *much cauſe to be diſpleaſed, themſelves (ſpecially* the more popular *) uſually taking the liberty of their*

Neigh-

Neighbours *Parishes and Pulpits upon all occasions, both without and* againſt the Proprietors *conſent.*

were not in the leaſt *edified.* Nor did they at all ſeek after *Baptiſm,* the neceſſity and benefit whereof *they were never taught.* Nor could they ſo much as repeat the *Lord's Prayer , Creed , or Decalogue,* becauſe the *Speaker,* attending higher Doctrines and *Speculations* (tho I take him for no *Fanatic*) did never acquaint them therewith: This and Catechizing, being with the generality (whom he was to *pleaſe, or all was gone*) quite out of Faſhion. Nor did theſe ſilly *Negro's,* ſo much as underſtand wherefore they were brought thither, it being never told them. The profound *Doctor,* believing his Reputation might be *diminiſhed,* if in his *Zeal* (of which *he was not at all ſuſpected*) he had condeſcended to apply any part of his Diſcourſe to them, ſo much as in *private,* but much more in *publique ;* which indeed *is the mighty dread* of ſome others beſides him. Whereby under *theſe great means,* the *Negro's,* who were quartered in the moſt diſtant part of their Meeting-place, remained ſtill as *brutiſh* as even *the more learned Engliſh ,* unto whoſe wiſer Capacities the lofty *Harang* was ſolely fitted and directed, without the leaſt *application* to the other. Who poor Wretches, apprehended (and, I believe, *truely enough*) their being brought thither to be no other than a *ſpecious* pretence, only to cheat them of their *Dance* and *Muſick,* and to abridg their *Liberty,* their other *work* being over ; (like thoſe who by their *zeal* for the *Sabbath,* do reap this great *ſpiritual* advantage of having their Servants thereby always in their eye:) They in the mean time eſteeming the *Church* for their *Priſon.* Which is no wonder, *our whiter People* (as we diſtinguiſh) *being much of the ſame Faith, touching going to Church, and Religion :* For otherwiſe our few

and

and narrow Churches could not upon Sundays even in the *Mornings* (for in the *Afternoons* we seldom Af-semble, as contrary *to the more laudable custom of our Colonie*s) amongst such multitudes of People, be so thin and empty. But notwithstanding from this *single Instance* (not to be parallel'd in all the *Plantations*, except in *New-England*) decrepit and simple as it is, they very roundly infer this general conclusion; *viz.* of the strange *Antipathy* of *Negro's* to *Christianity*. Which, (admitting it in any part for true) cannot certainly be greater, than *to Work and Labour*; and yet their *Taskmasters* have (notwithstanding) a *Faculty* to make them willing : And might no question bring about the other with equal facility, would they apply themselves to it, *with but half the industry and affection* they shew towards these. Nor is it likely that their *prejudices to Religion* (not, as I have often said, in the least discernable in any of them) should make them unwilling to part with an hour from the *heat* of the Field, to be spent in no harder Service, than *learning their Prayers*, with other necessary parts of *Religion*, at rest and *under the cool shade.* A priviledg never like to be obtained for them, whilst the World is so *rivetted* in our Peoples Hearts; who, would they but be *less good natur'd to themselves*, might find as great Instances (it may be much greater) of untractableness and *stupidity* even at Home, and amongst *Englishmen*; who yet must not therefore (and here I pray mark our great *Christian* partiality) be straightways reputed unmeet to be cal-led *Christians*; much less denied to be Men. But, even admitting the whole Charge, yet they might have fetcht this alleaged Averseness, from a more pro-bable and nearer Cause, *viz.* the *derision* with which themselves do usually entertain all Discourses about *Religion*, and their disrespect and barbarous treating of the *Ministers* of it; whereof these *Negro's* cannot

be

be ignorant. Tho possibly no less also from the same reason, for which the *Americans* are said to have *disaffected Heaven*, namely, the Cruelties exercised by the *Spaniards* over them.

§. IV. 1. But yet further to acquit themselves of all *Injustice* in this Point. (tho at no less rate than Blasphemy), they are not ashamed some of them to affirm, that the *Negro's* belief in the Deity is more *simple, pure,* and *sincere* than the Christians: Others of them do flatter themselves with a like wicked *Principle* of the *no necessity of Christianity,* in order to attain Salvation; whilst by a false *Key* of Imagination, they open Heaven Gates, and do very frankly bestow *Salvation* upon *Turks* and *Heathens* ; Accounting the contrary Opinion to proceed from the *ill nature* and peevishness of Melancholy *Religionists* and *Churchmen:* So also that the *Jews* believe sufficiently of *Christ,* by their expectation of the *Messiah* to come. And this I have heard maintained, not by our *Dunghil Wits,* but by the *Virtuosi* of the place. All which impious Conceits, do but bespeak their Malice against *Religion,* and at the best do seem to affirm no less than that *Christ's coming into the World, was either a Fiction,* (which he that openly proclaimed his— to be as honest a Woman as the *most glorious* and blessed *VIRGIN* , no doubt believed) or *to no purpose.* Thereby rendring the Preaching of the Apostles, and the Faith of all Christians

My indignation against these Blasphemies, forbids me to conceal them; the Authors whereof are Persons considerable for Place and withal the grand enemies of Religion, no less than of the Ministry.

(their own also, if they have any), to be but vain, if *Salvation may be had as well,* or *better without it.*

2. For certainly, were this true, it had been needless for St. *Peter* to have advised the Zealous *Jews,*

Acts

Acts 2.23. to Repent, and be Baptized every one of them in the Name of the *Lord Jesus Christ,* thereby to obtain Remission of Sins, and the Gift of the Holy Ghost. And our *Lord's* appearing to St. *Paul* before his Conversion, and then ordering him to address himself to *Ananias* (supposed to be the then Bishop of *Damascus*) to be told by him, τί με δ' ἐῖ ποιεῖν, *what he must do,* Acts 9. 6. had been no less idle, than the same Apostles preaching afterwards to others must also have been. And so His words uttered, St. *John* 15.5. *He that abideth in me,* &c. *For without me ye can do nothing.* And St. *Peter* to the Jewish *Sanhedrim,* had declared a very gross and palpable untruth, when to their Faces he positively declared, that *there was no Salvation* [to be obtained] *but by Christ,* if the same were no less attainable, not only by *Moses,* but by *Mahomet* also, or any other prosperous Impostor in *Religion.* And so likewise the Angel directing *Cornelius* to send for St. *Peter, who when he was come, should tell him, what he* MUST DO, (the very same that was by our *Blessed* Lord said to St. *Paul;* I say, that this) had been an evident *Delusion,* seeing there was no such Necessity of Christianity, as that impersonal [*Must*] doth import. And this of *Cornelius,* is a most pregnant Argument (and in truth unanswerable) both for the necessity of Christianity, and, I think also, of the *Ministry.* Who, *if ever any Person could,* might certainly no less have been saved without either. He being *one that feared God with all his House,* holding it in vain to be *Pious himself,* if he suffered his Family to be wicked. He was, as his Character declareth, Εὐσεβὴς, a *Religious and devout Worshipper:* One that *gave much Alms,* and *prayed to God always;* and at the 30th verse, we find him addicted to *Fasting,* a duty practised only by *devout* Persons: And for the certainty thereof, this we find all of it attested from

the

the Mouth of the *Holy Ghoft*, and by the Meffage and Confeffion of *an holy Angel*. But notwithftanding that *his Prayers were heard, and his Alms had in remembrance in the fight of God*; yet the main thing, the Knowledg of Chrift being wanting , St. *Peter* (our Lord refolving *to have his Work performed by its proper Minifters*) muft be fent for (the Angel *having no further Commiffion*) to inftruct him in that moft important Knowledg of Chrift. And for the *Negro's* belief of the *Deity*, St. *Philip*'s Preaching to the *Eunuch* by the like efpecial Mandate, fhews that his former *belief* was of it felf, and without this, *infufficient*, tho otherwife never fo *Pure, Simple,* and *Sincere.* Nor had there been any need thereof, if *Reprobated* and *Uncapable*, or naturally deftitute of any Right thereto. But that neither the *Negro's* fimple Faith, nor other Mens abundant *Charity*, nor yet the *Jews* Dreams of their *Meffiah* to come, can fave any Man tho living never fo uprightly therein; our Bleffed Lord's Anfwer to the *Samaritan* Woman, St. *John* 4. *Ye worfhip ye know not what, we know what we worfhip; for Salvation is of the* [true Church and Believers only, which are the] *Jews*, doth to me fully prove. Wherefore I fhall be bold to conclude this Point, in the words of the 18*th Article* of our Church, in which we find it declared; " That they are to be had Accurfed, that " prefume to fay, that every Man fhall be faved by " the *Law*, or *Sect*, which he profeffeth: For that " holy Scripture doth fet forth unto us only the *Name* " of *Jefus Chrift, whereby Men muft be faved.*

§. V. 1. Well, but if this will not do, they are fure that the next fhall; wherein 'tis pretended, firft, *That their Slaves are not hindred*, for that they may be Chriftians if they will: Secondly, That granting they were hindred, *yet that it would be no Wrong nor Injuftice to them*, for that at the worst, they could, thereby be but in the same condition here, in which they should have otherwise remained in their Native Country: And lastly, *That they neither seek nor desire it.*

2. To which I answer, First, That if it be true, that they indeed do not hinder them from embracing *Christianity*, they have then the less guilt upon them, and they are not to answer for so vile a Crime. Yet will not this excuse them, it being without doubt *their strictest Duty*, not only, not to hinder them, but to persuade and win them to become *Christians*; as I shall more fully shew, when I come to answer their third *Allegation*.

3. But secondly, As this Answer can no way excuse them, so neither indeed is it *true*: For to be plain, I must positively affirm, that they are *hindred*, and that more or less, these four ways.

4. First, By depriving them of *Time*, and denying them Persons to *instruct* them, and even imposing upon them a necessity *of planting Provision* for their Sustenance, even *upon Sundays.*

5. Secondly, By discouragements and *scoffs*, instilling into them a *slight esteem*, with an opinion of the *no necessity of Religion, as to Slaves and Negro's.* Which, next a desire of being Idle, (a Vice incident to our own People) is the cause of their avoiding the Room at Prayers (of which see *P. 9.*). Now *Scoffing* is term'd a *Persecution*, Gal. 4. 29. compared with *Gen.* 21. 9. Things *in their proper Nature* honourable, being apt hereby to be rendred *base and ridiculous.* And such a *Persecution* it is, as the most crafty Enemies of *Religion*, did hold it for the most effectual way to destroy *Christianity*; and as such was formerly no less dreaded by *Christians.* Nor can we blame the *Negro's*, if they contemn the *Religion* of the *English*, which they hourly

both

both hear and fee *trampled* upon, and *undervalued* by themfelves.

6. Thirdly, By direct force and punifhment of the *Innocent* Offenders therein, thereby to deter all others. Which in truth hath ftruck fuch a *dread* into them, that few have fince had the *Courage* to make the leaft offer at it. And fome, whilft privately learning their Prayers, dictated to them, have given fuch manifeft *Indications* of their *Fears*, that, as if *attempting fome Villany*, upon the leaft *noife* or *ftir*, their *Spirits* have failed them, and they have wanted Power to proceed, but were forced to give off, till the Coaft were clear, and they found that they might attend with more Security. And hereof 'tis eafie to produce divers Inftances, if required.

7. But there hath been a Force known to have been ufed, beyond *ill Looks, Frowns*, or bare *Words*; which 'tis certain was once (and for ought I know oftner) *without any great difcredit to the Author*, eminently, and, *in the face of the Sun*, executed upon a poor Wretch, offending in this kind. His Crime being neither more nor lefs, than receiving *Baptifm* upon a *Sunday-Morning* at his *Parifh-Church*, from the Hands of the *Minifter* thereof: Who was faid afterwards to excufe himfelf thus, *That he could not deny it, being demanded of him*. But the *Negro* at his return, did not efcape fo eafily: The *brutifh* Overfeer inftantly taking him to task, and giving him to underftand, that that was no *Sunday-work for thofe of his Complexion*; that he had other bufinefs for him, the neglect whereof fhould coft him an *Afternoons baptifm in Blood* (thofe I heard were his very words) as in *the Morning he had received a baptifm with Water*; which he accordingly made good. Of which the *Negro* afterward complaining to the fame *Minifter*, and he to the then *Governor*, the miferable Wretch was for ever after fo unmercifully

treated

treated by that inhumane *Devil*, that *to avoid his Cruelty*, betaking himſelf to the Woods, *he there periſhed.* An act exceeding all the Examples of *Turkiſh* Barbarity, and ſcarce to be parallel'd amongſt the *Immanities* of the moſt *ſavage* Creatures; who rarely (if ever) are known (unprovoked) to fall foul of, and to worry and deſtroy thoſe of their *own* kind; but contrarily, to defend them againſt the *violence* of otherlike, but different, *Beaſts of Prey.* The villanous *Author* whereof deſerved, beyond the Vengeance inflicted on *the perfidious Pedant of Falerii*, mentioned by *Livie, lib.* 5. to have been *whipt to Death* by the reſidue of his Slaves. Which notwithſtanding he has eſcaped, yet let him know, that *Divine Vengeance, tho it be ſlow, is ſure;* and that without a ſincere Repentance, attended with ſtrong endeavours *to repair this Injury* by him done to *God* and to *Religion*, there is a fearful Puniſhment reſerved for him; A *Baptiſm* alſo, not of Water, (or Blood only), but *in the Lake that burns with Fire and Brimſtone.* Nor here let any one by reaſon of the *horridneſs of this Fact*, ſtraightway therefore diſcredit the *Relation*, as impoſſible to be acted *amongſt Chriſtians;* the Story being rife in all Mens Knowledg and Diſcourſe, that *care to remember*, or take *notice* of it; and thoſe that do not, *being [here] unable to deny it.*

8. Fourthly, They are hindred by *muzzling Their Mouths*, who ſhould acquaint them therewith, and by rendring the Work very unſafe, even to the *Guides of Souls*, and *Miniſters of Religion*, which that *Quaker's Harangue*, recited in the Introduction to this Diſcourſe, as alſo the *Miniſter's* crude *Apologie* and *Excuſe*, (who *Baptized* that *perſecuted* and even *Martyred Negro*, I but now ſpoke of,) do enough imply. Who had he not been an *Eſtated* Perſon (a happineſs now not attainable)and no leſs ſtrongly fortified with ſreat *Friends* and *Relations*,

Relations, and withal an Ancient *Stander* (tho since fallen), he had for this been undoubtedly Ruin'd. And I am verily perfuaded, that none here befides *durst* to have done the fame : Nor, *I am confident*, would he himfelf have had the *Courage* to have *committed* the like Act again upon any other ; as by an *Inftance*, wherein he was fince concerned, I fhall immediately *fhew*. So that if our *Negro's*, who never underftood either the *Benefit* or *Neceffity* thereof (thefe being things carefully kept from their knowledg), in contempt of *Scoffs* and Difcouragements, their want of *Leifure* and *Inftruction*, and in defpite of the Overfeers *Rods*, fhall notwithftanding all thefe have a ftomach to be *Chriftians*, (without thanks to us) they may be fo when foever they will ; all thefe being reputed no *Impediments* thereto.

9. To this I fhall add the Barbarous Ufage of the *Preacher* before mentioned, together with the *Calumnies* and *fpiteful* Reproaches, wherewith they perfued him even to thofe places whither he retired to avoid their *Infolencies* ; of which 'tis certain, his *Sermon* (a part whereof, partly for his *Vindication*, and partly to let the World fee what kind of *Doctrine* it is they here much *Naufeate*, I have here Tranfcribed) was the chief, if not the fole occafion. Nor fhall I omit that when *another* had in difcourfe propofed fomething tending hereto ; his Propofal was fo malicioufly reprefented amongft the *Rabble*, that he told me, *he was endangered thereby*.

10. The fence whereof did fo much work upon one, whom alfo for his *character* I Pity, that he durft not give Chriftian Burial to a *Mulatto* Child born in his Houfe, and by himfelf privately (*tho not without importunity*) Baptized : The Father being of the *Scotifh* Nation, and the Mother his Domeftic Slave. For which reafon fhe muft be unmarried (*tho Baptized*);

I

left

left the Husband should thereby be *invested* with a propriety in her, and she should become no longer his; who was therefore compelled *to live in Fornication.*

11. For which cause also, when a certain *good natured* wealthy Person (and this is the Instance I promised) did *upon his death-bed*, make a Testamentary Alotment of some Weekly exceedings for Diet to six *Negro's*, during their Lives, in requital of their Fidelity and good Services to him; two *Ministers* (who successively came to visit him, and for whom he professed a particular kindness) being (in my hearing) pressed severally as they came, *to make use of the* opportunity, *and to try whether in that good Humour he might not be further wrought upon, so as to perfect and compleat his* Charity, *by a more necessary* provision *for their Souls, and perswading him to give* order *likewise for the instructing and* baptizing *of* those six Negro's; It was strange to observe how they were startled at this so unexpected motion; each of them giving manifest Indications of his inward Grief, but replying, *That as such* Proposals *were altegether* new *and* without precedent (O turpem notam temporum !) *so they thought it neither seasonable nor* safe *at that time* quieta movere, *nor to cause disturbance by such an* Innovation. *Neither did they judge it prudence thereby to* disoblige *their* Friends, *whereof they had not many in the* Island, *and to* exasperate *their Enemies. And being withal sensible what it was* to perish unpitied and unregarded; *and no less certain (even at the best, and supposing they should have the luck to escape a* grave *and insignificant* Rebuke *for their* indiscreet Zeal) *to be upon their greatest Sufferings, referred for their reward* to another World, *but never to hope for either* pity or compassion *from any in this.* And here we may reade the evil consequence of making *Ministers Annual Stipendiaries,* and of subjecting them to the *Arbitrary Talons* of *Vestries,* made up for the most part of sordid
Plebeians

Plebeians, the very Dregs of the *English Nation*, with whom to be truly *Confcientious*, is the height of *madnefß* and folly; and whofe difpleafure, even of any one of them, tho in the moft Righteous Caufe, doth portend the parties *moft certain Ruine*.

12. AND fo much for their firft *Allegation*: Now to the fecond I anfwer: Firft, That they are not fure but that by other ways, their *Negro's* Chriftianity might have been brought about, even in their own *Native* Country; where on the one hand there is a *freedom* and liberty of perfuading, and of *attending* thereto on the other; Advantages hardly to be met with, or to be *expected* here.

13. For, firft, It is not impoffible but that fome of thofe, whom we here do ufually reproach for *Madmen*, ('tis *happy for St* Paul *that he is dead*; for his very Chriftians would now not ftick to affirm him *befides himfelf*:) might in imitation of the firft *Difciples*, be (like them) poffeffed with *ardent* defires to enlarge the *Territories* of *Chriftianity*, and charitably to undertake Voyages thither for the *good of Souls*. Or that fome of thofe more fober and *wifer* Men, who travel for Preferment, and Wealth, might by fome chance or other be invited thither, as divers are: Where 'tis poffible, remembring the *WO to the unprofitable Servant*, and obferving fo much occafion and need in thofe parts for the *imployment* of their *Talents*, (with which *God had inftrufted them*); they might in time bethink themfelves, and laying afide (in fome meafure) the *ftudy of the World*, might more carefully addict themfelves to that true *Labour* for which they were appointed and *called*. Or, which one would think lefs unlikely; our *zealous Nonconformifts*, ftruck with thofe *Terrours* which they give out, for the reafon of their thwarting the *Law* at Home (where there is *no want of their Labours*)

con

confidering the much greater *Harveſt* in thoſe parts, might have reſorted *thither*, thereby to have convinced the World, that their pretences were *real* : and that the gaining of *Souls* to *Chriſt*, not the draining of their *Proſelytes* Purſes, and living in eaſe and *delicacy* in the Wealthier Places *only*, was indeed their great and mighty *Aim*, both in their *Preaching*, and other Actions of their Life : And there being in thoſe Countries both Liberty, (void of *Perſecuting* Laws and Magiſtrates, and free from the *Impoſitions* of *Biſhops* and *Ceremonies*) and Occaſion enough for even *thouſands* of them. Beſides, they ſhould, like *the Sons of the Prophets*, conſider that *their place where they dwell, is too ſtraight for them* ; and repleniſhed with others more ſuitable to the *Genius* of the Government, whereas elſewhere there is no *Confinement* to ſuch Inconveniencies. And this alſo would be a *noble imitation* of thoſe firſt *Chriſtians*, who when *Perſecuted in Judea*, fled into other parts, and there preached the *Goſpel*. Or fourthly, Some *Roman* Votaries, (they being of *thoſe that ſow beſides all Waters*) might out of their *Annual Miſſions*, be allotted for thoſe Quarters, and for ought we know are now preaching to their *Relations* ; whoſe condition as to *Religion* cannot be worſe; ſomething *bettered* it certainly may be, tho perchance not *comparable to what it ought*. And in all theſe caſes, 'twere hard if after ſo *much Toil*, their *Nets* ſhould ſtill be returned *emptied*. Eſpecially where thoſe irreſiſtable impediments to the growth of Religion, the *ſcoffs* and flirts of our *Witty Brutes* and Atheiſts, do not interpoſe to afright the more timerous and wary *Frye*, and to *hinder their Draught*. Laſtly, Some *poor Captive*, like the Woman carried into *Iberia*, or as *Frumentius* and *Ædeſius*, ſtrangers accidentally arriving there, might happily, by Divine Providence, have been the *Authors* of their converſion to *Chriſt* ; Nothing *in all this* being

impoſ-

impoſſible. And therefore they ſeem to Diſcourſe at random, and without aim, who affirm that our *Negro's,* tho here continued in their firſt ſtate of *Gentiliſm,* are yet in no worſe condition, than they ſhould have been in *Africa* ; and that therefore no wrong is done them. Indeed, had they been Tranſported hither, and here made *Chriſtians,* tho they had payed no leſs than their Liberty and *Quiet,* for the kindneſs, (to which they are forced *without it,*) I am perſuaded they had ſpoken nearer to the purpoſe.

14. NOR will their third *Allegation,* that *they neither deſire nor ſeek after it,* (to which, ſhould they go about it, they ſhould be ſure to receive that reply, which *Pharaoh* made to the *Iſraelites,* upon the like ſuit, *Exod.* 5. 17. *Ye are idle,* &c.) any more excuſe them, than the two former. It being a *Chriſtians* ſtricteſt duty, by his being ſuch, to perſuade and *invite* unbelievers and wicked Men, tho of a more diſtant and remote *Relation* to us, than our Slaves are, *to ſerve God,* and to embrace that Faith and *Religion,* by which himſelf doth hope to be ſaved, and without which he knows the other cannot. But if the parties be ſuch, as over whom he hath a *juſt* Authority, I there conceive it his Duty, if poſſible to *compel them to it* ; I mean by all fair and laudable means : As both the Parable of the *Supper,* St. *Luke* 14. and *Joſi 's* compelling *Judah* and *Iſrael to ſerve the Lord,* do manifeſtly prove. And therefore the *Patriarchs* in the Bible, tho their Servants ſought it not (poſſibly) any more than theſe, yet by their own Authority they initiated them into Religion. Hence *Abraham* whoſe honour it was, *That he would command* (and that certainly is Compulſion) *his Children and his Houſhold, after him to keep the Way of the Lord,* (and *in the ſteps of whoſe Faith each Chriſtian ought to walk,* Rom. 4. 12.)

is

is intimated to have *Inſtructed and Catechized* thoſe three hundred and eighteen, whom he led forth to *reſcue his Couſin Lot*: As may be ſeen by comparing *Gen.* 14. 14. with *Prov.* 22. 6. and their ſeveral Margents. And what he began, his Poſterity continued, whoſe *Slaves* were not only *Circumciſed*, but alſo admitted to the *Paſſover* ; which laſt were both by *ſpecial Command*, whilſt the other were purely *voluntary* ; yet commended, as *being alſo their Duty* even by the *Law of Nature*, and that Principle of doing good, ſo far as we are able, implanted in our Hearts. So alſo *Joſhua* reſolved, That *his Houſhold ſhould ſerve the Lord*, as well *as himſelf*. And *David*, Pſal. 101. purpoſed to retain none but *faithful* Perſons to *dwell in his Houſe*. And *Cornelius*, even before his converſion, or knowledg of *Chriſt*, is ſaid to *fear God with all his Houſe*. Without which, I fear, he had miſſed the character of being a *devout Man*. And it is no leſs evident, that in the *Goſpel*, the Faithful held it their *Duty*, even by virtue of their *Calling and Profeſſion*, to *Chriſtianize* their Servants. Every ſuch (even as Children and Subjects, are to Parents and Magiſtrates) being as it were ſo many Limbs and Members of their *Maſters* and *Owners*, and in ſome ſort the ſame to them as their *Children*, and no leſs accountable both to *God* and Man for them. From whence it may ſeem, That the ſame word in the three *learned Languages*, is frequently uſed to expreſs both a *Servant* and a *Son* ; to intimate that ſtrict care which each Father and Maſter had, and ought ſtill to uſe for the preſervation, and due proviſion for them, both as to Soul and Body, and for their *Spiritual* as well as *Temporal* Food. And for all others it is *Charity*, if not *Duty*, to keep Men *out of Miſery and Ruine*, even againſt their *Wills*. And tho they be inſenſible of it, ſhould they therefore be allowed to periſh, our ſelves beholding it, and not

adviſing

advising them of the *danger?* Should a *Physician* permit his *Patient* to starve himself, because he hath lost his *Appetite* through the viciousness of his *Stomach*, or over-long *Fasting* and *Abstinence*, and not be accounted (tho he escape being indited) for a *Murtherer?* 'Tis true, if after *due* provision made and tendered, he *rejects* it, and perisheth in that obstinate *refusal*, after all due Means and Arguments used to *convince* him, then we may say to him, *Perditio ex te ipso*, and the whole *guilt* of his destruction will lie *at his own door*. And therefore admitting it to be no wrong to the *Negro's* in not making them *Christians*, and that, what is before affirmed, they were of no probability of attaining to the knowledg of *Christ in Guinea*, which also is conjectural, and *but a mean commendation of the Traders* thither, (who, I have heard, *are by Bond always obliged to the contrary*); yet certainly we herein wrong our selves, by neglecting our *Duty* in so high a measure, whilst instead of performing *faithful service to Christ, to whom we have vowed our whole Man*, we in the mean time are found to serve the *Devil* and *Mammon* only. For, as the Orator testifies, that Person may justly be reputed an accessary to a Mischief, which *he might*, but did not *prevent*: Agreable to that of St. *James 4*. and the last ver. *To him that knoweth to do good, and doth it not, to him it is Sin*. And if Sins of *Omission* be by some accounted greater than those that are *acted* or done, there is no doubt but that he who *wounds his Soul* by omitting his *Duty*, injures and hurts himself equally with him that commits a *Villany*. Nor shall I be afraid to affirm, that if this I am speaking of, touching our *Negro's Christianity* being hindred (or at least neglected) be no Sin, then neither is *Perjury*, *Murther*, nor *Adultery*. And they, who, being concerned herein, do hold themselves innocent, may as safely presume that that *our Saviour Christ, to promote*

I 4

their

their Gain, will difpenfe with the moft palpable violation *of all his Laws.* For *Chriftianity* is a *Religion of Charity,* which teacheth us *to be Eyes to the Blind, Ears to the Deaf, Feet to the Lame,* and calls upon us *to open our Mouths for the Dumb,* and *which cannot Speak* in their own caufe. And it was *Chrift's* advice to *fell all and give to the Poor,* for the furtherance of *Chriftianity.* And if the Primitive Chriftians did from thence conceive themfelves obliged to difpofe of their *whole Eftates* for the fupport of *poor Believers,* and the *encreafe* of the *Church,* doubtlefs they were far from any *deduction* either from that, or from any other *Text,* for the obftructing it *for their private Gain.* Now 'tis all one *to forego our Profit* for the fame *good End,* as thus to difpofe of it when *acquired.* And that Piety is no lefs acceptable, which is the means of *introducing new Believers,* than of *preferving* the old. Nor is its worth at all *leffened* by the *quality* of the *Parties* won and brought over to the *Faith;* one *Soul* being as precious and dear to *God* as another, and a Slaves, being in his fight not inferiour to his *Mafters.* And where the confideration of the *End,* namely, *the good of Souls,* is the fame, the excellency of the *Duty* cannot be abated, by any *lefs worthy* intervening Circumftances. And this is to be underftood as relating to the care we ought to ufe for the *Salvation* of Strangers, living at the *remoteft* diftance, and without *relation* to us. But here is no fuch *plea* or pretence; tho it would be but of fmall *force.* The parties we fpeak of being their *Servants,* and even branches of *each Family,* by whom they in a manner wholly fubfift; (*fome,* and thofe not a few, *having by their Negro's labour* arrived to vaft Riches) and *for whofe Souls they are as certainly accountable to God,* as for *their own.* Who therefore cannot but claim a *fhare* equal with themfelves, in all things abfolutely neceffary for their life and being, and the

enabling

enabling them to perform *whatsoever* is by God or Man required of them. The detaining whereof, as St. *Paul*, 1 *Tim.* 5. 8. determins it, is no less than *a rejecting of the Faith*, *and makes the Oppressor become* WORSE *than an* INFIDEL. Whose calling himself a Christian, whilst (indeed) he is none, doth call to mind St. *John's* Censure, *Apoc.* 2. 9. of the like sort of People in his time, and gives us no less occasion to apply it here; *I know the blasphemy of them which say they are Jews, and are not, but are the Synagogue of Satan.*

Ezek. 8. 15.

Then said he unto me, Hast thou seen this, O Son of Man? Turn thee yet again, and thou shalt see greater Abominations than these.

CHAP.

CHAP. III.

That the Inconveniencies *here pretended for this Neglect being examined, will be found no-thing such, but rather the* contrary.

§. I. n. 1. THE *absolute* neceffity of a *Chriftian's* pro-moting *Chriftianity*, even in defpite of the greateft Difficulties and Inconveniencies being fhewed, I come now in the laft place to examin thofe very *Inconveniencies*, and to try whether they are in-deed fuch, as they are *pretended*; or whether the con-tinuance of thofe practices for whofe *Juftification* this Plea was invented, will not upon a due trial be found more *inconvenient* and prejudicial to our *Intereft :* At leaft whether *Chriftianity*, notwithftanding thefe *pre-tences* (whether true or falfe) may not, upon the fcore of its *innocent* deportment, and unqueftionable *blamelefsnefs* in all Ages, without the leaft hazard to any Man's *juft Right and Intereft*, be afforded a free courfe, and find entertainment amongft *all* Conditions and Degrees without *prejudice*, or *offence* to any.

2. And here I fhall not *conceal*, what I have often within my own Breft *confidered* and *wondered* at ; how, and with what *Front* thefe Perfons who proclaim to the World, the *inconveniencies* and dangers threatned by *Chriftianity* to their *Eftates* and *Lives*, (for *no lefs are the things in controverfie*) can utter things which I am certain themfelves neither do, nor can, *believe :* It be-ing impoffible but that Men endued with *common fence* muft know (and that with the *higheft certainty* that they can have), that nothing of prejudice can *really*

accrue

accrue to any Man by the *Christian Religion*. But much less can they be imagined ever to have entertained any thoughts touching a *future Account* to be given for such *blasphemous suggestions*, which to the dishonour of their *blessed Redeemer*, and his *Eternal Truth*, they continually belch forth *without the least shame* or *blush*. For otherwise Christianity might doubtless have found more *candid* and *civil usage* from them, than to have thus put upon her such an *hideous* and *frightful* Dress, as these have taken the *boldness* to represent her in, unto the more ignorant and besotted *Herd* of *Mankind*, in these *remote* Quarters of the World.

3. For it cannot but appear evident, even to the dimmest and most bleared *sight*, that no such extraordinary *danger* can possibly attend the *Work*, I am here suing for, on our *Slaves* Behalf; there being no persecuting *Magistrates* carrying in their Brests an *hostile Enmity* against either the *Professors*, or *Promoters* of it; nor yet breathing out *slaughter* and *destruction* to them. There are no Confiscations of *Estates* or *Goods*; no loss of *Liberty* threatned; nor is it a *Crime* now to be a Christian; the *Civil Powers* being such themselves, and *Kings* and *Queens* being long since become *Patrons* and *Nurses* of the *Church*.

4 Yet notwithstanding this, they are not ashamed to infer ('tis true, not always in express words, as I have said) even as great *Mischiefs* from their *Negro-Slaves* becoming Christians (but not otherwise) as the *Faithful* in the Primitive Times sustained from the most persecuting *Heathens*. It being their common *Affirmation*, That the *Baptizing* of their *Negro's*, *is the ready way to have all their Throats cut*, &c. which my self, and I believe thousands of others have heard declared and insisted upon by them, with *much vehemency* and *indignation*; tho without any great shew of *Reason* to make it out. For being at any time demanded,

manded, from whence those *fears* could arise, they should never fail most perti-

So Turtullian *saith of the* Gentiles, Nolentes audire, quod auditum damnare non possint. *Apol. c.* 1.

naciously to *persist* in the Affirmative, *That it was so.* Which, with the addition of a few *angry* words, and *uncivil rude speeches*, in reply to those demands, thereby to testifie their displeasure thereat, as well as the danger of enquiring further into their *secrets*, was what was usuall to be *gotten* from them.

5. But that which I have casually learned from certain *False-Brothers* of the *Society*, hath in their more retired *Cabals*, been alledged by them (and which indeed *was no other* than what I before *suspected*) was principally these three things.

6. First, They object the *Knowledg wherewith their Slaves would be thereby furnished*; which they are sure will make them less governable, and like the *Galileans* of old, or our *seditious Reformers* in 1642. to *mutiny* and *rebel*, to free themselves from *Tyranny* and *Oppression :* Possess them with the *Quakers*, (of whom here are great numbers) and other *Phanatic's spirit of Obstinacy*, against all Laws and Government, and *dispose them rather to suffer Death* than *to be subject*, and at last *out of pure Conscience, to murther their Masters.*

7. Secondly, They object *the charge* and *loss of Time*, viz. *from their Sunday-work*, &c. with divers other the like *sore Inconveniencies*, which in the end will (forsooth) strike *deep at their Profit*, and quite ruine their *Estates.* And therefore they often repeat this saying, *If the* Negro's *get to be Baptized*, they *must then e'ne take the* Island *to themselves.*

8. Thirdly, They complain that the *Terms of Christianity are in some things too large*, but *in some other too narrow for them*; both ways inconsistent with the condition of Bondage: And therefore that their *Negro's* are

are not to be admitted to, nor entrusted therewith. In which three we have a brief *Account* of both the *Principles* and *Men*, that are such fierce Enemies to this way of propagating *Christianity*: Their *Religion* and *Interest* are of one and the same piece, nor *are they ashamed to own it to the World*. Doubtless, these do conclude the *Merchant* in the *Gospel*, who judged it worth his while *to sell all that he had* besides, to purchase *that Pearl*, to have had but a very shallow Pate, for *setting such a high* value upon *nothing*, or at most, but *Toys* and *Fooleries*, whose worth they believe lies only in the *fancy* and *opinion* of the Wearer, not in any *intrinsic excellency of their own*.

9. But to undeceive the more well disposed, and to defeat their Malice by unfolding this *Mystery of Anti-Religionism*: I shall in answer to their first *Objection*, here demand of them, of what kind that *Knowledg* is they stand so much in fear of? Is it the knowledg of *Vertue* and *Goodness?* Certainly it cannot be other which Christianity instructs Men in. And how can there arise any *danger* from such knowledg should they receive in never so great a proportion? Can the *Decalogue*, *Creed*, and *Lords Prayer*, with some few *Catechistical* and general Points of the more necessary parts of Christianity from thence deduced, prove so poysonous to the minds of Men, as to make them deserve a Character due only to the vilest *Blood-suckers*, and cruel *Assassins?* Or can *these* be a means to render them *suspected*, or *dangerous to the World*, when 'tis known that nothing but the *non-observance of them*, is the sole *occasion of all*, as well the greatest as the least *evils?* And therefore the *Slaves* Right understanding and instruction in these *Doctrines*, can no more be a motive to him to *slacken his Duty*, or prejudice his *Master*, than an *Artizan's* known skill in his *Trade* can unqualifie him for being imployed therein, or his tried *Honesty*,

from

from being either trufted or dealt with. This knowledg therefore muft in common Reafon, be concluded
to be the *Mafter's* chiefeft *Intereft*, being indeed a worthy inducement to the *higheft truft and confidence* in his
Servant, thus endued therewith, and no lefs ought to
be his *firft care*; That is, to make him *Juft, True*,
and *Honeft* to himfelf. At leaft, none can reafonably
be the more fufpected for addicting themfelves *to fuch
a Study*, which only directs to *Integrity* and *Vertue*.
Where though they may be thought to begin *but in
Jeft*, yet 'tis probable, they may *end in Earneft* : Their
Reafon may be overcome by the force of its *Arguments*,
or elfe their fight may be captivated : For, *Vidit hanc,
vifámq; cupit*, doth here very often follow ; the *thorow underftanding of Vertue* (as *Plato* obferved) *being
apt to create moft ardent affections to it*. Nor can any
genuine, or *true principle* of Chriftianity, give the leaft
occafion for either *Fears* or *Jealoufies*, becaufe in their
own proper nature *the moft innocent and oppofite to all
Frauds, guileful Practices, and worldly Policies, of any
Religion ever yet profeffed or taught*. Thofe *Crafts* and
Circumventions, which the generality of Men *do not once
fcruple*, being moft loathfom to the Mind of a true
Chriftian. And therefore it is moft evident, that no
Mafter can be endangered by his *Slaves* inftruction
therein, which thefe *Blafphemers*, who affirm the contrary, cannot but *know* ; unlefs we will fuppofe them
like *Owls* and *Bats*, to be ftark blind in the cleareft
Meridian light ; and that amidft all the *Books* and *Sermons*, with which this *latter Age* hath been fo abundantly ftored, any Man can poffibly ftill remain fo
ignorant, (tho *fubtile enough as to other lefs commendable
and excellent* things) as to be utterly unacquainted,
with the firft and greateft points of his *Religion*.

9. But here withal, I muft confefs, that I am not
of their mind, who hold none fit to be admitted for
Chri-

Christians and *Members of the Church*, but Gifted, Wife People only. Such as are able to *Extemporize* an hour or two, and *fpeak to a Text*, as they call it. This poffibly, as being of that *kind of Knowledg or Science* which may be apt to *puff them up*, might in its confequence prove fatal: It being not to be wondred at, if their fwelling Tympany of *fancied Abilities* do make them prefume, fince we read that when *Hagar*, (a Bond-Woman too) *had conceived*, fhe foon began to behave her felf impudently *towards her Miftrefs*. The knowledg therefore which I here plead for, *is fuch as tends to their Edification only*, being of things *abfolutely* neceffary, as of *God*, our *Bleffed Saviour*, and of the *Holy Spirit*; of *Faith*, *Hope*, and *Charity*, and of *Repentance*, of living *uprightly*, and of a confcientious difcharge of their Duty *both to God and Man*. And if thefe can be *hurtful*, then I fhall not be afhamed even with the *Adverfaries* to confefs, that the knowledg of *Chrift's Religion*, is a thing Repugnant, and Inconfiftent with the moft *honeft* and juft *Intereft*, and wholly tending to *difturb the good Order and Peace of the World*. And yet here I would not be mifconftrued, as if intending to *abridg* any Mafters *kindnefs* to his *Slave*, who hath a defire to furnifh him with greater knowledg: Only my requeft is, *That he would not damn him for the want of this*; which as I am fure it is *fufficient to fave him*, fo neither is it *confiderable enough*, for *his Mafters fears*. And fo much touching this *firft* Point, viz. *The danger arifing from the* Negro's *knowledge*.

10. The fecond is an Implication of the fouleft charge againft *Chriftianity*, which the worft Enemies of it did ever fuggeft, but could never prove, *viz. That it inftigates Men to Mutiny and Rebellion*: Which cannot poffibly be true of it, but by *Principles directing thereunto*, therein contained and taught. Which if fo, then 'twere impoffible for a Chriftian not to be a *Rebel*; and

and the better *Chriſtian the more Rebellious.* But unto ſuch *Practices* nothing is more diametrically oppoſite, than the genuine Doctrines of *Chriſtianity.*

11. For firſt, It preſſeth *abſolute* and entire *Obedience* to *Rulers* and *Superiours*, as may be collected from almoſt innumerable places of Scripture ; but more eſpecially from the 13*th* to the *Romans*, and from St. *Peter's* and St. *Judes Epiſtles.* And our Lord's anſwer to the *Herodians*, is ſufficient to ſilence all Cavillation touching this Duty. It gives the Title of *Gods* to *Kings* and Magiſtrates, forbidding ſo much as to *ſurmiſe evil of them.* And this is ſo plainly and evidently true, that amongſt *Atheiſts* and *Commonwealths-Men*, (*two Names for one and the ſame thing*) it is the only Crime known to be by them charged with, *viz. That it inveſts Governours and Monarchs with ſo independent and abſolute a Power.* And thereupon *have for divers Years paſt*, wiſely endeavoured the *ſuppreſſion of it*, to prevent (what they are pleaſed to term) *Tyranny* and *Slavery*, and in order to the *advancing the liberty of the Subject.*

12. Secondly, It eſtabliſheth the *Authority of Maſters*, over their Servants and Slaves, in as high a meaſure, as even themſelves could have preſcribed ; in a a due proportion placing them in a no leſs *abſolute degree of Power*, than the former. Exacting the ſtrictelt *Fidelity* ; and that without any reſpect to their *Quality and Condition*, but of their *natural and true Right of Authority over them.* Requiring ſervice *with ſingleneſs of heart, as unto the Lord, and not unto Men*, Epheſ. 6. 5, 7. And ſo far it is from encouraging Reſiſtance, that it allows them not the *liberty of Gainſaying*, or making undutiful replys to their Maſters. And referring them to *future recompence in Heaven*, for their *faithful ſervices done to them upon Earth*, Eph. 6. 8. Of which Ties and Promiſes, *Gentile* Slaves being deſtitute,

deſtitute, no ſuch *Fidelity* can be from them hoped for, or expected. And ſo far is this *Religion* from a tendencie to *Anarchy,* or any *Levelling Tenets* (as being *founded not in a Parity, but a Superiority,* not in a *Domocracy,* but in an *Ariſtocracie*) that a conformity to that *Axiom, Æqualitate nihil iniquius*; *Nothing is more dangerous than Equality*; has been her moſt profeſſed and *conſtant Practice* from her firſt appearance *untill this very day.*

13. Thirdly, It enjoyns to all in general an *abhorrencie of evil,* tho ſuch only in *appearance.* But much more prohibiting thoſe things *which are plainly ſuch,* and even of the groſſeſt and wrankeſt kind. It further puts a reſtraint upon the *Thoughts* and Deſires, which no other Religion doth; forbids us to be *revengeful,* or to *return evil.* And therefore far out-doeth the *Heathen Divinity,* which permitted *Revenge in caſe of Injury,* allowed in no caſe amongſt Chriſtians. So that whoſoever can pick *Rebellion,* or *cutting of Throats* out of theſe Principles, may as eaſily prove *Adultery* lawful from the *Seventh Commandment,* or *Slandering* from the *Ninth*; reconcile *Contradictions,* and bring Contraries to *concur* and *agree* in all Points at one and the ſame time.

14. And therefore the Deluſions of thoſe *Atheiſts,* and *Impoſtors* in 1642, and afterwards, (ſince declared, *viz.* by the *Parl.* in 1660, to be no *Proteſtants,* and as certainly no *Chriſtians*) to whom *Chriſt* will one day return but ſmall thanks for *occaſioning his Doctrine thus to be blaſphemed*; can be no ſuch convincing Argument, that their *Murthers* and *Depredations,* tho *falſly* pretending *Scripture* and *Inſpiration* for them, were the *genuine reſult of Chriſtian Principles*; until better Proof and Reaſons for it be produced, than their own bare Affirmations. And for the *Galileans action,* it was (like other of the ſeditious attempts of that *Nation,* both before and after to *aſſert Liberty*)

K   but

but a *Jewish Dream*, which *Christ* himself did to their no smal indignation plainly disown, and in that his answer to the *Herodians*, St. *Mat.* 16. utterly *condemn*. And for the *Quakers* obstinacy (whom yet they *here support* and *incourage* against the *Ministers*) I know no further nor better use can be made of it, than *from thence to infer the necessity of Church-Government, and of suppressing false Opinions in Religion*, from whence this Obstinacy is occasioned and derived, But not therefore to stifle and hinder Men from the knowledg of that *Profession* and Truth, which teacheth the contrary. But our People, who in truth have as little stomach to *submit to others*, as they believe their *Slaves* have to submit to them, will scarcely be brought to approve of this *Use*, or *Inference*. Tho these *Quakers* refusal to bear Arms, and to defend their *Island*, (no not in case of an Invasion) together with their *Commission dormant* of *New Light* and Revelation, *reserved against some fit time* and *opportunity* of Action (whereby no Man is secure) do often put them upon thoughts of *using Violence* to that their own dear principle of *Libertinism*, no less than to the others *tender Consciences*.

15. Lastly, For *Insurrections* and *Revolts*, nothing can be imagined a greater *Security* against them, than a sincere inward persuasion of the truth of *Christianity*, with a thorow *knowledg* of its Principles. Of which the effects have been lately seen in *New-England*, where their *Christian-Indians Fidelity* was tried to the uttermost; encountred on the one hand by the *jealous surmises of their Friends*, and on the other by the both invitations and threatnings of their Enemies, if at least we may so term their *unconverted* Country-men : Yet *in despite of all*, they remained *firm to the English*. Who, *after that they durst trust them*, became very serviceable to our People there, as hath been attested by more than one of their *Writers*. So powerful are the Bonds of Religion to unite the minds of Men, tho of most

different

different and even contrary *Interests:* And when sincere and hearty proving *indissolvable,* tho under the darkest *Eclipse* and trial of *Adversity.* Making Men to *forget their own People, and their Fathers House,* and joyning them in affection to the most *distant Strangers.* For these having so fair an opportunity of *Revolting,* and all the invitements and arguments for it, which Men upon such occasions could wish for; as, the ridding their Country of *Foraigners,* and the enriching themselves with the *Spoils* of their well-built and better furnished Houses; their *Lands* manured and stored with *Cattel,* and abounding with many other conveniencies, which themselves never were blessed with: And lastly, the *Royetlets* and several *Tribes* of that *spacious* Continent, all in a manner up in Arms, and *unanimous* for the *rooting* them out of it. Yet none of all these considerations could prevail with those *Indians,* whose minds were thus seasoned with *Religion,* to falsifie their *Faith* once plighted to the *English.* With whom doubtless things might have gone *much harder,* had they been *deserted* by them. And they might perchance (*all things considered*) have been glad to leave their more *Inland Stations,* and forced to retire and betake themselves to their greater Strengths on the *Sea-Coast;* there to have remained *pent up,* and despairing ever to recover their *lost Territory,* but by the aid of *extrinsic* force, which would (probably) have cost them more, than *they are willing to part with.* And to come a little nearer, even to our own *Island,* where 'tis possible that the late *Plot* had not been so near taking effect, had the greater, or indeed any considerable, number of the *Negro's* here been *Christians.* One thing more I shall add, that the *Spanish Indians* in *America,* are not recorded once to have rebelled since their first *Reduction* under the *Spanish* Power; nor have the Conquerers themselves been disturbed with any

In

Intestine Broyls, that have been confiderable ; which is more then we can boaſt of in our *Colonies,* tho feated (I ſpeak even of the *Eldeſt of them*) not above one third part of the time, that the *other* have *enjoyed* theirs. Which effect I can aſcribe to nothing more, then to the force and power of *Religion.*

16. But there is one *Inſtance* worth all that can be *produced,* or ſaid upon this Subject, and that is the Example of the *Theban Legion ;* which I ſhall preſent in the words of a *Modern Author*.* "It is, *faith he,* one "of the nobleſt paſſages in "all the Eccleſiaſtical Hiſto-"ry, wherein Chriſtianity "did ſhine forth in its full Luſtre, and it affords plen-"tiful Light for our inſtruction. This band conſiſted "of almoſt 7000 Men, all Chriſtians. The Empe-"ror *Maximian* commands the whole Army to offer "Sacrifice to falſe Gods ; they remove their Quarters, "that they might avoid, if it were poſſible, this occa-"ſion of diſcontenting him. He ſummons them to "perform their part in this deviliſh Worſhip. They "are forced to return an humble denial, and their re-"ſolution not to diſobey God, for whoſe ſake they "had ever been, and would continue faithful Servants "unto him. The Emperour unſatiſfied with this An-"ſwer, puts them to a *Decimation.* They ſubmit with "much Cheerfulneſs, and die, praying for their Mur-"therers. After this ſad Spectacle, his Commands "are renewed ; but prevail nothing upon the *Remain-*"*der ;* wherefore they are all Butchered without the "leaſt reſiſtance. There was no delay in their Death, "except from the wearineſs of the Executioners. "This was truly to confeſs him, *who was led as a Sheep* "*to the ſlaughter,* and *like a Lamb opened not his Mouth* "and they a Flock of his Fold, are quietly devoured

* *Mr.* Dudley Diggs, *of the unlawfulneſs of Subjects taking up Arms againſt their Prince,* &c.

"by

" *by ravening Wolves.* The Commander of this Regi-
" ment *Mauritius* could not contain his joy, when he
" had feer the firft Decimation gallantly fuffered. How
" fearful was I, faid he, to his Fellow Souldiers (for
" armed Men may be tempted to defend themfelves),
" left any of them upon colour of juft refiftance for
" felf-prefervation in an innocent Caufe, fhould have
" ftruggled againft this bleffed Slaughter, I was watch-
" ful, and had *Chrift's* Example in readinefs, who
" commanded his Difciple *to put his Sword into the*
" *Scabbard.* *Salus veftra non periclitatur, nifi armis ve-*
" *ftris ;* If you ufe not your Weapons, *I have God's own*
' *Warrant for your fafety.*

17. " Defpair it felf could not conquer one fingle
" Patience, which yet creates valour in Cowards, and
" makes them more couragious in Extremities, be-
" caufe they are Fearful ; fince they are likely to en-
" deavour moft to preferve Life, who are moft terrified
" with Death.

18. " But it may be objected, *Vires deerant,* they
" were not able to go thorow with the Rebellion. This
" very Objection, *faith he,* was made by the Ancients,
" and anfwered by themfelves to our Hands. Their
" Speeches witnefs fufficient ftrength, if Religion had
" not tied their Hands. Which had they been other than
" truth, muft have armed their fo potent Adverfaries
" with fufficient *Arguments* againft them.

19. The fame *learned Author* goes on, and tells us
that, " St. *Cyprian* faith exprefsly, *Quamvis nimius &*
" *copiofus nofter fit populus ;* Tho we have competent
" Forces enough, yet we wreftle not with our Oppref-
" fors. The *Theban Legion* was in a pofture of refi-
" ftance, but they durft not lift up thofe hands, into
" which the Emperour had put Weapons, againft his
" Perfonal Commands, tho unjuft and bloody. Six
" thoufand fix hundred fixty fix Men, of fuch extra-

K 3   " ordinary

" ordinary Valour, as did not entertain the leaſt fear
" of Death, might probably have conquered, (and
" this Cruelty might have encreaſed their Party, by
" the defection of Male-contents) at leaſt they muſt
" certainly have made ſome ſport for their Lives:
" They could not have wanted that Comfort, which
" to ſome taſtes is beyond the pleaſure of Life, *to die*
" *revenged.* Beſides, had not the Emperour and his
" Council known them *true Chriſtians,* and been acquain-
" ted with the tameneſs of that Profeſſion towards the
" Higher Powers, he would never have hazarded a
" Rebellion, by making ſo conſiderable an Army de-
" ſperate.

20. " And *Tertullian, Cui bello idonei non prompti fu-*
" *iſſemus, etiam impares copiis, qui tam libenter trucida-*
" *mur ;* How could they poſſibly receive a Foil, tho
" ſhort in number , who ſo quietly do ſuffer our
" Throats to be cut ? *Numeri damnum virtus penſaret,*
" tho we wanted the advantage of number, which you
" perceive we do not, Courage would ſupply that de-
" fect ; And tho fewer, ſince we contemn our own
" Lives, we might be Maſters of yours. We could
" undo you, not if we ſhould Rebel, but if we would
" be Idle ; we were loſt, if we did not Fight for you.
" *Veſtra omnia implevimus, caſtra ipſa,* &c. We fill all
" places in the Empire, and even your Camp would
" be empty without us *Chriſtians.* The ſame Father
" makes a bold Challenge, and deſires them to pro-
" duce, if they can, but one example of any *Chriſtian*
" taking part with Rebels. Their unanimous Con-
" feſſion was, We kiſs the Hands that wound us, and
" the Example of Chriſt is made our Law. *Inde eſt*
" *quod nemo noſtrum, quando apprehenditur, reluctatur, nec*
" *ſe adverſus injuſtam violentiam veſtram, quamvis nimi-*
" *us & copioſus noſter ſit populus, ulciſcitur.* For this cauſe
" none of us makes reſiſtance, when apprehended, nor
" revengeth

" revengeth your unjust Violence ; for God is able to
" reward our Patience, and to requite all our Suffer-
" ings. *Si injuriam*, &c. If you depend upon God,
" he will undertake your Quarrel, and revenge your
" Wrongs ; your Wounds shall save you : and if you
" fall a Martyr, you shall rise a Saint. What cannot
" our Sufferings do ? They make even God our Deb-
" tor ; He owes us Heaven for our selves, and Hell
" for our Enemies, but we breath out our Souls in
" Prayer, that he may be entreated not to pay this.
" Here is the Patience and Faith of the Saints ; they
" believed, therefore they suffered such things, *&c.*
Thus far that *loyal* and *ingenious Person*, in whom is
legible the *genuine temper* and *spirit of a Christian* : Unless it can be supposed that the whole multitude of
them, *as well their more learned Guides*, as the ignorant
and simple, were wholly unacquainted with their *Profession.* And from hence, with what else-where hath
been said, I may safely presume to conclude, that *Christianity which obligeth Men to the strictest Vertue*, and that
upon such weighty Motives, as no Profession did ever
pretend to, *is so far from working Mischief to Superiours
and Governours, that it rather appears of absolute necessity
for the security both of Themselves and their Affairs, that
their Subjects be thorowly acquainted with it* ; As, er'e
I come to close up my Discourse, *I hope, I shall yet
further shew.*

§. II. 1. The first and great *danger* which concerns
their *Lives* being escaped, I come to examine the *two
last* Objections, which for their near *affinity* and resem-
blance, I shall twist together, and dispatch under one.
These do concern their *Estates* and worldly *Interests*,
things no less dear unto them ; but both dearer than
Religion ; for otherwise such Objections had not been
to be answered. Now in the first they affirm, Their

Estates

Estates will be threatned no lefs than four feveral ways; of each of which I fhall give this fhort, but true Account; *viz.* That, the firft *is Idle and Ridiculous*; the fecond *Sordid and Unchriftian:* The third a *mixture of Gentile and Mahumetan* Superftition and Irreligion: The fourth *Inhumane and Monftrous, a reproach to Mankind,* and a *difhonour to the Englifh Government and Nation.*

2. For the firft, They affirm their Eftates will fuffer by the *Charges* from hence enfuing: As by *Baptizing, Marrying, Churching,* and *Burying* their *Slaves.* All now either totally omitted, or elfe performed by the *Overfeers,* (in a kind of prophane Merriment, and derifion as it were of the Ordinances), or (as in Marririage) by mutual agreement amongft themfelves; and (as is ufed jeftingly here to be faid, when fpeaking of the *Quakers* (like) Marriages) *after the Negro fafhion.* As for *Vifitation of the Sick,* I fhall not infert it in the Lift, becaufe here laid afide in a manner by all, befides *the richer Englifh.* The other (like *thofe poor defperate Souls in Limbo, that for wont of Money,* have no Body to pray them out) being by the remotenefs of their Habitations, the frequent *badnefs* of the Weather and the Ways, the *fcarcity of Minifters,* an *evil, but little felt, tho much fewer,* (notwithftanding *there are not above five*; and the numeroufnefs of the *Inhabitants* (fuppofed not fewer than one hundred and odd thoufands) not poffibly to be thought on, unlefs we fhould fuppofe the Minifters always on Horfe-back for that very work: And then *who fhould preach (without Book) upon Sundays?*

A County in England of the fame extent with this Ifland, has commonly 100 or more Parifhes and Minifters; all, one with an other, not worfe provided for Maintenance, tho not a quarter fo Populous *nor* Rich *as thefe here.*

3. Secondly, They apprehend that this would produce a *neceffity of enlarging their Churches,* and encreafing

the

the *number of Parishes* and *Ministers,* of both which there are but too many already, *half of the Churches being destitute of Ministers,* tho but *Eleven* in all. And in those Churches that are better supplied, 'tis known that the *Prayers and Sermons* are usually delivered to *little more than the bare Walls* only, notwithstanding the multitude of People belonging to each; of whom not a fifth part (*I speak only of the English*) could be admitted into most of them, *should they all appear.*

4. Thirdly, They add the time to be spent in this (needless) *work of Religion,* which amongst so many *labouring Hands* must be considerable. Besides their *Sunday-work* would be quite lost, as also their *increase by the Negro's Polygamy.*

5. Fourthly, They have a strange apprehension and foresight, *that their Slaves when admitted* Christians, would be apt to expect better usage (*which even Heathens will tell them they ought to have without it*) for *Food, Clothes,* and *Rest,* and more *merciful Correction,* moderated according *to some Law,* (and not left to each Tyrants pleasure) which perchance, *may be but reasonable.* These, as indeed the former, they sparingly mention, being ashamed *to own,* and it were to be wished they would also to *practise,* them. Of all which I shall leave others to judg, whether they do not fully answer my short *Character* and *Description* of them.

6. But as *bad* as these are, the following *are worse;* wherein like down-right *A-theists,* they stand up for *Libertinism,* and object directly against Christianity, blaming the equability and justice of its Terms, the thing that chiefly renders it commendable.

Luc. l. 9. Olim vera fides-- obit, nunc & ficta perit. They declare their Sin as Sodom, Isa. 39.

These they complain of, as on the one hand too large, but on the other too straight and narrow, in neither able to content them, being both, they say, in-

inconfiftent with Bondage. Thefe Terms are, 1. Privileges. 2. Prohibitions.

6. The *Privileges* are chiefly thefe three : Firft, Their *Slaves admittance to an Oath,* which, being at prefent *Heathens,* are fcarce currant *in a Chriftian Court* ; as fome of them have been made to underftand in *England* from a certain Judg's *reprehending* and *menacing* of them for their brutifh neglect herein; tho they were not *ignorant* of it before. Secondly, Their *equality as to the Communion* and *Church-Adminiftrations* ; which, to all are, or ought to be, the fame. Thirdly, The *inconvenience* that may enfue upon their acquaintance with this Precept of our Bleffed Saviour; *Thou fhalt love thy Neighbour as thy felf.* It may perchance be expected that I fhould add a fourth, *viz.* A *fuppofed Right to Freedom,* and *of being fet at Liberty* immediately upon their *Baptifm* ; which is by fome apprehended to be in it felf *a releafe from Servitude.* To which laft, (tho it be needlefs, they having fecured that *Intereft,* as I have underftood, by a Law of their own, whofe *Validity they do not queftion,*) I fhall fpeak fomething alfo, after having firft replied to the three former.

7. The firft whereof is their *admiffion to an Oath,* wherein they feem again to have forgotten, the thing I am interceding and fuing for on their behalf, *viz. That they may be made Chriftians* ; which, as is before fhewed, is certainly of it felf a fufficient remedy and fecurity againft *all temptations to Perjury.* A *Crime,* which according to the true Principles thereof, *is next to irremiffible* : And for which the *Ancient Canons* did enjoyn Penance to the Offender during *his Life.*

8. And yet fhould we fuppofe the worft, I cannot imagine the danger to be greater than it was in *former Ages,* when both *Slaves* and Villains were freely admitted, without this fcruple, to give Evidence ; even as in *Poland,* and elfewhere, 'tis not to be doubted, but they

they still are. Nor do I conceive that St. *Paul* thought his *Christian Slaves* Oath more to be suspected than other Mens, whilst they no less stuck to the Principles of *Christianity*. And in truth, at the same rate, all the World may be no less suspected : it being possible that all Men may prove deceitful and wicked, tho not in the least probable.

9. That their *Oath may be useful,* we even now find, where their bare word or testimony given without it, is often found very serviceable, tho not admitted for a sufficient proof. The want whereof is many times no small *impediment* to the *course* of *Justice*. And for *Subornations,* the thing chiefly objected ; for my part, as I see not but they might (especially being made *Christians*) be as well trusted as most others ; so should any such thing happen, it will be presumed that the *wise Judges* will be no less *Eagle-sighted,* and able to descry such practices in these, than in the *English.*

10. As for the second, it is hard to find out what they intend by it, unless it should be that the *Negro's* would thereby be apt to think *more proudly of themselves,* and less worthily of their *Masters* ; which yet cannot be gathered from *Christianity,* nor indeed can ever happen, if St. *Paul's* rule be well applied ; *And they that have believing Masters, let them not despise them, because they are Brethren, but rather do them* [the better] *service, because they are Believers,* 1 Tim. 6. So that this *Authority* of the *Master* is so far from being hereby diminished, that it is rather confirmed, and a stricter observance for that cause charged upon the Servants *Conscience.* Nor do we find that *Abraham, Job, &c.* were the less esteemed by their *Bondmen,* for their being initiated *into Religion,* by the same *Ceremonies* with themselves ; neither do we find or suspect this in our *English* Servants, or Dependents. That Woman also whose *Negro* (P. 38.) I baptized, had not more cause

to

to complain that he thereafter failed in his *Duty* and *Fidelity*, tho she quarrel'd at it. Nor yet two others in *Virginia* (the former being in *Carolina*) whom I likewise Baptized, were ever taxed by their *Masters*, as less diligent after *Baptism*, than they were before. Nor lastly, did the *Hebrew* or *Christian Masters*, nor I believe hardly any other Sect, ever ascribe to *Religion* the disorders of their Servants as the cause thereof, if at any time they found themselves disrespected by them. Except only the *Romans Saturnalia*, wherein the Slaves were permitted to retaliate their Masters cruelties ; which extravagancy *Christianity* doth not in the least allow of. And for the *third*, they may remember, that if Christ hath taught, *That we should love our Neighbours as our selves*, his Apostle hath from his Mouth also, no less enjoyned *Servants obedience to their Masters* ; which two *Precepts* do no more thwart either the other, than that of the same Apostle, commanding, To *render to every Man his due*, and *Masters to allow their Servants that which is just and equal*, doth destroy their just Right and *Authority* over them. And this, if we were to deal with Men that had any sense of *Christianity*, or *Religion*, (which the Objection doth most evidently shew that they have not) might prove satisfactory to them ; but as the case stands, 'tis not to be *hoped* will much avail to their *Conviction*.

12. And as to that which some would in the *fourth* place object, touching their release from servitude upon *Baptism*, tho I do not see that they here do retain any *apprehensions* thereof, their *Law* (of which I have only heard mention here, but do know that there is such both in *Virginia* and *Mary-land*) having carefully *barred all such Pleas* ; yet were there no such Law enacted, I cannot understand that a necessity for such a release doth arise from any Principles of *Christinity*, nor of *Religion* in general. For if we look into

the

the Old Teſtament, we find that *Circumciſion* (to the Faithful then the ſame with *Baptiſm* now) did not re-leaſe *Abraham*'s three hundred and eighteen Slaves, nor thoſe afterwards belonging to his Poſterity, any more than *their partaking of the Paſſover*, Exod. 12. did; of which yet *no hired Servant was to eat.* And the *Gibeo-nites* were perpetual *Bondmen* and *Vaſſals*, notwith-ſtanding their admittance to the *Temple*, and to *Reli-gion.* And then to come to *Chriſtianity* and the *New Teſtament*, *Oneſimus*, who is ſtiled [Δȣλος, a Slave] (to *Philemon*) as (, that word importing no leſs) is generally agreed, was not made a Freeman by his be-ing *Baptized*; which S.*Paul*'s returning him to his Ma-ſter, a *Chriſtian* alſo, and his interceeding for him, doth manifeſt. Whom tho he beſpeaks as a *Convert*, yet lets him know that his Obligation to his *Maſter* was ſtill the ſame. And tho he profeſſeth that he might be much bold in Chriſt to enjoyn *Philemon* that which was convenient, yet that he choſe rather to entreat him by Love: And what was that? Not that he might be ſet at liberty, as being now a Chriſtian, and *even a Bro-ther*; but that, forgetting wherein he had offended, being now a Penitent and a *Convert*, he would *receive him* again. Nor againſt this do we find *Oneſimus* urging his Privilege, nor refuſing to carry the Letter with his own hand. A manifeſt ſign that there was then no ſuch underſtood, or heard of. And in 1 *Cor.* 7. 21, 22. where the ſame St. *Paul* aſſerts the privilege of Chriſtian Servants, he withal tells them their Duty, giving them to know, that they were *to abide in the ſame Calling, wherein they were* when firſt converted, or *cal-led*; not but that if they could procure *their liberty, they ſhould rather uſe it.* And if any ſhall demand **what** then is that liberty of a Chriſtian, which St. *Paul* elſe-where aſſerts and urgeth? I anſwer, That I know no more by it, than a *liberty from the yoke of Judaiſm*, from

Sab-

Sabbaths, Circumcision, and such like Ordinances and Levitical Ceremonies. As also a release from our former slavery to our *Lusts,* which is the greatest liberty and happiness, if considered and understood. And lastly, An admission *to serve Christ, our most perfect Freedom,* and to partake of the Privileges and Promises of the *Gospel,* and thereby to obtain an *Adoption to the glorious liberty of the Sons of God in Heaven.* Which certainly are far greater Immunities, than a bare release from temporal Servitude can possibly amount to. For *Christ's Kingdom* being not of this World, his *Religion* was never designed to deprive any Man of his *civil Rights,* but rather did *confirm them all to us.* And to shew that *Bondage* is not *inconsistent* with *Christianity,* we see it practised by other Christian Nations in these parts without the least prejudice to them: Even as not one hundred Years since in *England, Villanage,* a kind of *Slavery,* was in force, and still is in other Countries; and some do say, in our own too.

13. And whereas 'tis further Objected, That certain *Canons* and *Imperial Edicts* (neither of them admitted here), and the *Municipal Laws* of some Countries ('tis possible of *England* it self) heretofore enacted or decreed for the honour of *Christianity,* or to strengthen its Party against the *Heathen,* do oppose this continuation of our *Slaves* in Bondage. I answer, First, That these Laws being designed for the good of Servants, and the promoting of Christianity, there is now no reason they should be continued, when *experimentally* found, through *the hardness of Mens Hearts,* so great impediments thereto; and even to be turned against them, *for the benefit of whose Bodies and Souls they were intended.* But, Secondly, I add, that this (tho true) doth not trouble my Assertion, because we do not find that these Laws do flow from any necessity thereof, concluded in the Principles of Christianity;

as

as being meerly *voluntary*, and the effects only of the good Nature and Piety of their first Christian Contrivers ; and to which a Christian (as such) is no more bound, than to *sell all his Goods, and give them to the Poor* : Which yet may be a good work, and very commendable, in those that shall aspire after such perfection.

14. But yet further, if any shall make it a matter of *Conscience* to continue Christians in Servitude ; it would concern those that entertain that scruple (which I fear few do) to remember how much more against a good Conscience it is, either through Sloth, or for a petty Profit, to keep *Men, that have Souls to be saved,* destitute of the means thereto, and consequently *to occasion their Damnation* ; than simply to retain them under Servitude, abstracted from that other *Irreligion.* Which tho perhaps less commendable in *Christians,* is far short of the Impiety of keeping them *Slaves to Hell,* and to *our selves too.* And here also, supposing the worst, it ought by Christians to be considered how much the loss of a *Servant* is less than of a *Soul,* (yea of many) *for whom Christ died,* no less *than for their Masters* ; and who cannot expect to be *saved,* if the other, *through their occasion,* perishes. But letting this scruple pass, (to salve which there never will be here any occasion), I think it clear enough that *Christianity* doth not lessen any obligations of Servants to their lawful *Masters* : And therefore that if any *positive Laws* to the contrary do as yet stand in their way, I should be apt to recommend the *Bermudian caution* of *Indentures* for 99 years Service, to our Peoples *imitation,* in the *interim* till those Laws (I say, if any such there be) might by *Authority* be fairly removed.

§. III. 1. And thus our dangers from the *Privileges* being cleared, I proceed to do the like by the *Prohibitions,*

tions, *viz.* Of their *Polygamy*, their *Sunday-Labour*, frequent *repudiating* and changing their Wives, usual amongst most *Heathens*. As also their *Idolatrous Dances* and Revels, permitted and practis'd by them (so often as they can steal any time from their Work) *even upon that Day*, whose *Morality* (to the danger of straining it to the height of a *Jewish Sabbath*) hath been so much, for these many Years, insisted on amongst the *English*; with other such *Recreations* and *Customs*, by them brought out of *Africa*, and here connived at, because either *gainful to their Owners*, (such as the first) or grateful to the *poor Slave* (such as the latter) *without prejudice to their Masters Business*. None of which yet are heard of amongst the *Virginia Negro's*, tho alike *Gentiles* with these : And there not laid aside or forbidden, but forgotten by disuse.

2. Now might not this cause one to stand still and to admire, how such things should come to be, I do not say, *justified*, but even permitted, or endured by Christians : Who, as before they were not ashamed to begrudge the poor Wretches *thus spending their strength and days in their Service*, even a miserable Subsistence, for they expect no more : So here they alledge things palpably wicked, as a pretence for a worse and more dangerous *Frugality*, if I may so call it, *viz. The starving of their Souls*. Contenting themselves to give a free course to *Turkish* and *Heathenish* Licentiousness, and even to all *Irreligion* and *Atheism*, for a wretched false Gain ; but in the mean time *blindly overlooking the many greater Advantages, which are the undoubted fruit of true Christianity*.

3. For can it be believed that the small trouble of *Christenings*, to be had without *Fees*; as also of *Catechizing*, *Marrying*, *Churching* and *Burying* of them (the consenting to *which* will one Day, like *Nehemiah*'s good deeds for *Jerusalem*, or *Tobit*'s charity for the Dead, be

our

our greatest comfort ;) can equal, or any way be compared with the solid benefit and satisfaction arising from the unquestionable *Fidelity* and

Think upon me, O my God, for good according to all that I have done for this People, Neh. 5.

Integrity of a vertuous Servant ? Can a few hours *Sunday-Work* (for I plead not for the other *Holy-days*) be alike beneficial to us, as the same spent in learning them their Duty, or *as the blessing of God* upon us for it in the ensuing Week ? Can *starving, or working them to Death,* (for it cannot be denied but that these are too frequent) be equally *profitable with keeping them alive* for our future Service ? Or can we believe it alike expedient, or conducive to our *Interest*, to be put each Year to purchase and train up *Raw, Ignorant,* and unhandy *Barbarians,* with preserving for our *occasions,* the tried and more experienced, by good *usage* of them : 'Tis true, you may alledg the temptation and *certainty of the present Profit,* with the uncertainty of *future Contingencies,* the possibility of their out-living those *hardships,* and of their dying also under *better usage* ; yet surely this is but a *brutish Plea,* and at best not a little favouring of their *Providence,* who *devour all at one Meal, as uncertain whether ever they should live to enjoy another.*

18. As for the charge of *Instructing* them, if they think it too much to undertake themselves, (which the *holy Patriarchs* did not) they cannot but know the same Person who attends this work upon *Sundays,* or *Saturdays Afternoon,* (which last was formerly allowed to both Slaves and Servants, when this *Island* was less Wealthy and Populous, than now it is) may be further useful in the rest of the Week ; particularly in teaching their *own,* and the neighbouring *Youth,* (or possibly in keeping their *Accounts,* &c.) which would prevent a greater Charge, together with the hazard

L   of

of tranſporting them to *Europe* for *Education* : Not omitting that ſo much (beyond the *dangers* of the *Sea*, and of different *Climes*) worſe miſchief of their being betimes *Debauched*; ſcarce to be avoided at ſo great a diſtance from their *Parents care and inſpection*, as in many Inſtances is too apparent. And this alſo might be a means in ſome meaſure to put a ſtop to that *Barbariſm*, which through the want of *Schools*, do threaten the irrecoverable *Ruine* of all our *Hopes in them*.

19. As for the danger of our *Slaves releaſe from Servitude* thereby, to what I have ſaid before, I ſhall only add, That if they ſuſpect the *Validity* of their own *Laws*, the contrary to which I have always found; no doubt but his *Majeſty*, and the Honourable Houſes of *Parliament*, will have their Ears open to their juſt Fears and Complaints, thus ariſing from a pious ſenſe of their *Duty*, and the ſafety of their Peoples *Souls*, no leſs than of their own; ſo as to fortifie their *Intereſt* with as good Laws and Fences, as themſelves ſhall in *Reaſon* propoſe, or their *Omnipotencie* (pardon the expreſſion, *Rulers* can do much within their proper *Spheres*) can *create*, or give life to. Nor let that over-proud fear of thereby acknowledging (*what they cannot poſſibly avoid*,) their dependence upon *England*, nor that of rendring the reſt of their Laws, with their *Legiſlative Power* (which, I confeſs, ſome would fain extend beyond its *due bounds*) queſtionable, be any impediment thereto; ſince neither the one nor the other are more *ſecured* without it : And theſe two being known to be *different things* in Law, *viz. To corroborate an old*, and *create a new Title*.

6. And for the charge of dividing and leſſning the *Pariſhes*, (very neceſſary if but the for *Engliſh* alone) and the encreaſing the number both of *Churches* and *Miniſters* (tho this doth not abſolutely follow; the

fore-

foregoing *Expedient* being admitted , nor perhaps without it ;) All the danger which from thence is like to arise, is, that thereby we are like to be made better *Christians*, and by such a convenience *enabled more duly to serve God*; a benefit well worth the *purchasing* at so small an *Expence*. Tho *Christians* in such a case should first reflect upon the *Prophets* reply to King *Amaziah*, 2 Chron. 25. 9. *The Lord is able to give thee much more than this.* And the old *Jewish Aphorism*, *Decima ut dives fias*, answering to our English *Adage*, that *Meat and Mass*, (others have rendred it, *Prayer and Provender*) *do never hinder Work*, do confirm that in the Sum total, *Nothing is lost by our attending upon God's Service and Religion.*

7. Hereby also, besides the *Integrity* and *Long-livedness* of their *Slaves* (which would abundantly recompence the loss of other less commendable *Profits* and Advantages), their gettings would not be so clogg'd *with those troublesome gripes*, and *stings of Conscience*, which first or last are the certain *Appendices* of *unlawful* and *bloody* Gain; nor with that *Curse* denounced by the *Prophet*, *Hab.* 2. 6, 7, 8. for such Unmercifulness and Impiety. Nor would their *Estates* be so subject to that Moth and Canker, which some observing Persons (not *over addicted to Priests*, nor to *Religion*, 'tis well known, but) even from amongst themselves, have (so *forcible are Right words*, Job 6. 25.) been brought to confess, as being most *Notorious* : Who at the same time could not find out any cause whereto to ascribe those apparent effects, besides *that of oppressing these People*. For as an *Achan*, or a *Saul* may trouble *Israel*, so even very *Gibeonites* may *bless the Inheritance of the Lord.* And so all would be enjoyed with greater Security : And that which now is as *unstable as Water*, and a *Curse* rather than a *Blessing*, would be a *durable and firm Possession*; not as now for the most part to the *immediate*

Heirs

Heirs only, but even to the *succeffion* of many Genera-
tions : For as one very well obferves, " *Intereft is beft*
" *preferved by Juftice and Equity, which will entitle it to*
" *that bleffing from God, which he hath promifed in his*
" *Word, and which are naturally apt to be inftrumental to*
" *Providence in producing that good, which he hath pro-*
" *mifed.*

8. And as each *private* Man, fo alfo the *public*
will be made more happy. *Religion*, faith one, *cau-
feth good Orders, and good Orders do create Peace and
Concord*, which is a Peoples greateft ftrength. *A Fool,
if he tread in the ways of Holinefs and Religion cannot err*,
according to the Prophet *Ifaiah* 35. 8. *There fhall
be an High-way and a Way, and it fhall be called the Way
of HOLINESS*; *the wayfering Men, tho Fools, fhall
not err therein.* And on the other fide, *Baalam* hired
to procure the ruine of *Ifrael*, could not devife a more
pernicious Counfel, than to make *Ifrael fin.* *Livie* in
his fifth Book, rehearfeth a fpeech of *Camillus*, to the
Romans, wherein he appeals to their own Experience,
whether ever they had better Luck, *than when they
carefully ferved God, or worfe than when they neglected it.*
So *Horace* alfo in his *l. 3. Ode 6.* And *Cicero* afcribes all
the good fortune of the fame People (and no lefs doth
St. Auguftine in his Book, *De Civitate Dei :*) to their
Piety and Devotion. *Nec numero Hifpanos, nec robore
Gallos , nec calliditate Pœnos , nec artibus Græcos ; nec
deniq; hoc ipfo hujus gentis & terræ domeftico nativóq; fenfu
Italos ipfos & Latinos ; fed Pietate ac Religione, atq; hac
unâ fapientiâ quod deorum immortalium Numine omnia regi
gubernariq; profpeximus , omnes gentes Nationéfq; fupe-
ravimus ;* That is, *We* [Romans] *neither outnumbred
the* Spaniards, *nor were ftronger than the* Gauls, *nor out-
witted the* Carthaginians, *nor were more learned than the*
Greeks, *nor furpaffed the* Italians *and* Latines, *our pre-
deceffours in their natural Capacities :* But by our *Religion,
Piety,*

Piety, and by this one only point of *WISDOM, that we believed all things to be directed by the appointment of Heaven, we have been able to worst all other Nations.* *Xenophon* tells us, That the great *Cyrus* laid not the foundation of his *Persian* Monarchie so much by his Valour and *Wisdom,* as a *Religious* Worship of *Heaven,* and a liberality even to profuseness in the service thereof. This also was that which did aggrandize *Alexander* the founder of the *Macedonian* Empire. And hence it was, saith one, That the *Romans* made not an unworthy choice of a Commander, or *Officer,* for many Years; the way there to be preferred, being by *Religion.* Therefore this became the grand *Emulation* of the People, *Souldiers, Captains,* and *Senatours.* And *Comines* was persuaded, that hereof did spring the greatness of the *Venetian* Seigniory. From thence *Matchiavel* admonisheth those *Princes* and *Republic's ,* that would keep themselves from Ruine, above all things to preserve the Rights of their Religion uncorrupt, and to *maintain it always venerable.* And he further adds, *That there is no surer sign of a Countries destruction, than to see in it a contempt of Divine Worship.*

9. Before I can conclude this part, I must crave leave to recite another memorable passage out of *Livie's* first Book of his *Roman History,* as conceiving it pertinent to the Point I am upon : It being touching the effects of *Religion* upon *Rome's* first *Planters,* for that also was a *Colonie.* Whom in the first place, he bespeaks to have been a *People rude and savage :* But to abate whose *fierceness,* and to render them more tame and mansuete; *Numa* their second King, endeavours by good *Laws and Orders,* to reduce them to *Civility,* thereby as it were to reedifie that City, *whose Foundation had before been laid by Force and Arms.* Howbeit this being too little to accomplish his purpose, (*a thing worthy to be taken Notice of;*) He in the next place,

L 3

devifeth

deviseth *to bring them to some sense of Religion*, and *the fear of God* ; *Rem omnium primam ad multitudinem effi-caciffimam ratus* ; *judging this above all most operative upon the generality of Men.* Whereby, as it follows, their Minds *poffeffed with an awe of Religion,* A folemn *promise* and the *respect of an Oath*, did, *without further Laws or Penalties, govern the City.* Nor was the bleffing from abroad attending their Devotion, lefs remarkable. For, faith our Author, This *Piety* obferved in them, did fo affect their Neighbours: *Ut civitatem totam in cultum verfam Deorum violari ducerent nefas* : *That they judged it Sacrilegious to vex or moleft a People, fo addicted to the Service of God.* I fhall leave our People to make the *Application,* without adding any thing more thereto, than what our *Lord Chrift* replied to the *Inquifitive Lawyer,* St. *Luke* 10. 37. *Vade & tu fac fimiliter,* Go *and do thou likewife.*

Ezek. 8. 17.

Then faid he unto me, —Is it a light thing— that they commit the Abominations, which they commit here ? For they have filled the Land with Violence, and have returned to provoke me to anger: And lo they are [ὡς μυκτερίζοντες] *like them that make Sport or Mock.*

CHAP.

CHAP. IV.

Wherein certain little *Shifts and Pretences from* England *are examined, and found weightless. Also some few Proposals preparatory to this Work are laid down ; with Exhortations to both* Ministers *and People, to a chearful and speedy betaking themselves thereto.*

§. I. n. 1. MY three *General Assertions* being finish'd, I should with them here draw to a full *Conclusion,* did not an *Objection* or two from the further Shore oblige me to the contrary. Where (as I have heard, it was not long since *threatned* from another place, and is since fallen out, tho not upon the occasion which they desired, as a pretence for it ;) it is feared that the *enforcing* hereof (as if *nothing less* could be used) would go near to endanger a *Rebellion,* and is therefore believed less safe to be attempted, especially in *case* it should not succeed. Secondly, They suppose The *time to be unseasonable* ; the *Jews* pretence, *Hag.*1. Thirdly, That since they cannot yet compass to *settle Religion* at Home, how should they hope to accomplish any settlement in those remote parts ? So that here are no less than three terrible *Lions in our way* to this work : Of all which yet, if well lookt into, *David's* words, *Psal.*53. will be undoubtedly verified, *There were they in great fear, where no fear was.*

2. For, First, It is to be considered that the *disproportion* between these two, is as wide as between the setting up of a *Cottage* and a *Palace,* or the building of St. *Paul's* and of a Country *Church* : Where he that wants sufficient *Strength* and *Materials* for the one, may

L 4   yet

yet be amply furnisht for the other. And here also is the same difference as between a *Being* and a *Well-being*; which those that shall be apt to *envie* the last, will blush to *deny* the first; this being by all granted necessary, which is the utmost of our wishes here. Besides, there the *Dissenting Parties* are at enmity with, and do oppose that settlement, who yet, I doubt not, would all of them put their helping hand to this: None besides direct *Atheists* (and I hope *our good People here will pardon me for this*) daring to object against it. And, *for the Time*, the Prophet *Haggai* has answer'd it to my hand, in the *Chapter* before mentioned. And so much shall suffice for the two last Objections.

3. Now to the former, I shall answer, That as I hold our Planters and Merchants *Interests* too great in *England*, ever to betray them into such a folly as a *Rebellion*; so I presume the ill success of it elsewhere, and the less probability of better here, where most of their substance is imported from *Foraign parts*, would be enough to prevent all such *Attempts*.

4. But were our security against such fears *greater* and the danger *less*; yet, I must confess I am not for *forcing*, but *persuading* our People thereto, by good *Sermons* and *Pious Books*, preached and wrote upon that Subject: And no less by encouragements from the *Government* (where it ought to begin) to both *Ministers* and *People*, who should be most forward and industrious therein. 'Tis I know out of Fashion with the *English*, to prefer Men for Religion, but only for Craft and Wealth, which is the cause that things do so happily succeed with us. Whereas the *holy Scripture* (as also the practice of the wiser Heathen) will teach us that the *Magistrates* properest qualifications are *Piety* and *Temperance*; such only as *feared God*, *Men of Truth*, and *that hated Covetousness*, being to be advanced to that Dignity. Now if this course were taken

ken

ken, besides that it would cut off all *pretences* for Stirs and Commotions, this design could not fail of making a considerable progress in a very short time. Especiall, knowing how grateful a thing *Power* and *Honour* is to our thriving *Planters*, and how *Ambitious* they are to catch at every shadow of *Title* or *Preferment*.

5. But next thereto will be the procuring that this Impiety be taken notice of and decried at Home, especially in *London*; where they have an extraordinary *Ambition* to be thought well of. This, alone, if well understood, and for some time carefully kept up and managed, would operate and strike deeper into them, than even St. *Paul*'s 14 *Epistles*, together with the *Sermons* and *Comments* thereupon, of a thousand Years past and to come.

6. Yet since that this last must in all likelihood be difficult to be brought about to any great purpose, our old *English Zeal* being so much *abated*; I shall go a nearer way to work, and propose some few things, which shall concern, 1. The *Ministers*. 2. The *People*.

7. Concerning the *Ministers*, (and here my Brethren will, I hope, take no offence, their Infirmity and Failure herein being so long since proclaimed by the Pen of that *Quaker*;) I shall propose first, That each *Minister* invested with the **cure of** *Souls*, be in his particular Station strictly obliged, once at least each Month, to press this Duty from a *suitable Text* unto his charge; not omitting the same at other times. But, *Secondly*, That above all things they be especially *Exemplary* therein in their own Families, by Instructing and *Catechizing* their *Slaves*, and in due time admitting them to the *Sacrament* of *Baptism*.

8. Concerning the People, I shall propose only, That each *Owner* possessed of a *baptized Slave*, be obliged to allow him the free and full Exercise of *Religion*, without compelling or suffering him to *practise* his former

Gentilism

Gentilism. And that to hinder a Slave from being *Baptized*, or to moleſt any *Miniſter* for doing that charitable Office; or, after this, to deny him the Exerciſe of *Religion*, ſhould be a preſent and abſolute releaſe to the ſaid *Slave* for ever.

9. But then in order hereto, it would be convenient, and even highly neceſſary, that the *Miniſters* (I ſpeak not this for *my ſelf*, as having no ſuch *Charge*, and being reſolved ſo to continue, till they) be *freed* from their *Veſtry* dependences, by a *ſufficient* Maintenance (for which the alone *reſtitution* of their *Glebes* would in ſome places ſuffice,) and ſettled in their *Benefices for Life :* For otherwiſe they ſhall paſs their time in perpetual *fear* of *offending*, and to be afterwards Checkt and Starved for *conſcienciouſly diſcharging their Duty.* And that there be ſome Regard had and proviſion made for them of (at leaſt) a Subſiſtence upon their return, after ſome convenient time, into *England.* (The Miſſionaries into *Mary-land* being, as I have heard, always ſent for after 4 Years continuance there ; their Superiours thinking it too unreaſonable to oblige them to a longer abode.) There being not the ſimpleſt Curate there, whoſe hopes (without any hazard) are not greater, than they can poſſibly be ſuppoſed here. And it being againſt reaſon that any innocent Man ſhould, as if for ſome great Villany, be condemned to perpetual Exile amongſt a People utter Enemies to his Profeſſion, and even worſe than Strangers. And laſtly, That ſome one Perſon or more, be conſtituted as Agents for each Colony, to repreſent

For what Encouragement is it for Men to put themſelves into the Public Service, and venture their Lives and endure Miſery, when they ſhall but thereby deprive themſelves of thoſe Opportunities (which others at Home ſhall ſeize) of which perchance they were certain, had they been preſent : And after this to be lookt upon but as Vagabonds at their return ?

present the grievances of the Church and Ministers to the Government in *England*, it having been hitherto found to very little purpose to make Complaints here. Witness that Scoff of some Members of the, *&c.* in reply to the Ministers Petition,

I speak not this as reflecting so much on the Place, as the usage: For, as the Poet wish't,

—Neq; enim miser esse
  recuse :
Sed precer ut possim tuti-
  us esse miser.

bidding them for shame to put it up in their Pockets, least the *Quakers* (whose abuses they complained of) should see it and laugh at them; which was all the Redress they then did, or are since like to get. Besides all this it would be but just, that all *Scoffs* at *Religion*, should be prohibited upon severest Penalties. That our Slaves *Polygamy*, with their *Sunday-work*, be restrained, no less to those that remain *Heathens*, than to such as shall become *Christians*. That so that *filthy Lucre*, (which is indeed the same with *Theft*, or *Sacriledg*,) may be no longer a temptation for continuing them *Heathens*; nor their being *Heathens* be made a pretence for that *Irreligion*. Which preparations being once made (and without them all will be nothing), the work afterwards will go on smooth and *easie*, and even in a short time prosper into a *Perfection*: As ere this it might have done, had not the *opposition* of such *who believe that* Labour *may well enough be performed without Religion*, stood in the way.

10. Nor will the generality of the People be disatisfied therewith, when they shall understand it to be not more their *Duty* than their *Interest*: Some few of them having been discoursed already into this acknowledgment, That in regard *Religion* would be apt to *create a Conscience* in their Slaves, it might be convenient, *in order to make them the truer Servants*. If this were frequently inculcated unto the many, with the hopes of other advantages together inspired into them, no

doubt

doubt the *Majority* would soon be wrought into a *Compliance*, and even the reft obferving the bleffed Fruits thereof, would become lefs fturdy in their *Oppofition*. Nor can the *Government* be other than pleafed thereat ; confidering the great fecurity, it will above all other *Intereft* affuredly reap thereby.

§. II. n. 1. Wherefore, *Be ftrong, O* Zerubbabel, *faith the Lord, and be ftrong, O* Jofhua, *the Son of* Jozedeck, *the High Prieft, and be ftrong all the People of the Land, and Work; for I am with you, faith the Lord of Hofts* ; as the Prophet *Haggai, Chap. 2. 4.* fpeaks. And let both *Minifters* and *People* encourage and *provoke each other to Love and to good Works.* Let the *Minifters* fet before them the *Religious Profeffion* of holy *Job,* declaring his *efteem for the word of God's Mouth, viz.* the work of *Religion, to be more than for his neceffary Food.* But efpecially the Example of their B. *Mafter, whofe Meat it was to do the Will of him that fent him, and to finifh his Work.* And with the great St. *Paul,* let us be evermore *preffed in Spirit, and ftraightned in our Bowels,* at the thoughts of thefe Peoples deplorable Eftate ; Not only the poor *Barbarians,* from whom the *Key of Knowledg is kept, and who are hindred from entering in,* but the *Englifh,* who are the *Authors* thereof. And as *Miltiades* Victories did fo inflame the emulous mind of *Themiftocles,* that he could not reft for them ; fo let the Memory of others more glorious *Atchievements* in this kind, provoke in us the like pious Emulation, not fuffering us to *give fleep to our Eyes, nor flumber to our Eyelids,* until we have arrived within a profpect of its accomplifhment. Let us confider, that we have no more *Difpenfation* for our filence than the *Apoftles,* with other fucceeding holy *Bifhops* and *Priefts,* had, who firft planted and watered the *Church* with their Blood ; and went about, and *preached every where,* when it was

death

death to be a *Christian*. That Faith is an active and prolific Grace; and cannot remain in Idleness, but must operate and imploy that Heavenly Heat which it receives from above, for the use of others. That there is no *Neutrality* in this War, and that whoever is not actually in *Arms* prepared to fight *against Sin* and *Infidelity*, is to be reputed a *Conspirator* with them. That there is the same Heaven and Salvation proposed for the conversion of *Slaves*, as of more illustrious *Grandees*; the whole being but the *saving of Souls*; the effecting of which upon but a very few, is worth the Labour of many, all their lives. Even *we*, no less than St. *Paul*, are *debtors to the* Greeks *and* Barbarians, *to the Wise and to the Unwise*. And God hath by an extraordinary *Providence*, brought these People to our very Doors, to try our *Justice*, and to see whether we will pay his Debt, unto which, if ever any did, each Soul of us do stand most *firmly* obliged. Look upon them, and you cannot but see in their Countenances the lively *Effigies* of St. *Paul's Macedonian*, imploring your help: And, O! let not the *blood of Souls cry from the Earth* for Vengeance *against us*. Reflect but upon the sad Doom denounced *against* the *fearful and unbelieving*, Rev. 21. and remember that the first great Founders of our *Faith* were no *Cowards*. Think what a shame it is, that we have given such just occasion to the *enemies* of *Religion*, to reproach and triumph over our *Timiditie*, or, which is worse, our temporizing for *filthy Lucre*. And since,

——*Fas est & ab hoste doceri*, and that the bitterest Reproaches may have a *salubrious Energie*, when prudently applied; let us view the Charge (drawn out of our own *Liturgie* against us) and from thence learn to prevent a *second*; and by wise endeavours for the redeeming of our past *Errors*, give undeniable proofs of the *deep sense* we have of this *Duty*. Nor are we to

slight

slight those *puny* Adversaries, but to reform our selves ; remembring that of *Solomon*, *Prov.* 29. 1. and also 12. 1. which I shall not repeat. And if it can be possible for an *Heathenish* indifferency to

And that of Cicero, Negligere de se quid quisq; dicat non solùm arrogantis est, sed prorsus dissoluti. *l. 2.Off.*

harbour in so much as but one single Brest of any devoted to *a nearer* and more peculiar *Service of Christ* in the Ministry ; yet let his *Prudence* teach him to throw his *Garment* over that part of *his Nakedness*, and to try at least to conceal it from the World. And, *Si non re ipsa dolet*, If he cannot be passionately concerned, *dissimulare certè est Hominis*, it would be his Wisdom not to betray himself, nor disgrace his company. Especially in this day of Rebuke, when the *Mouth of the Slanderer* is opened, thus bidding us *defiance.* Nor let the opposition and peevishness of *unreasonable Men* dishearten us ; as knowing that our true portion is to be sent forth *as Sheep amongst Wolves* ; and that success is for the most part the companion of a restless Industry. *Nothing*, as the Wise Man saith, *Prov.* 27. 4.

* *As also* 2 Kings 18. 31. & Isa. 37. 32.

(see the * Original and *Greek*) *being of force to withstand* Z E A L. The Stars, they say, cannot exercise their Influence upon the *sphere of Fire:* And certainly the *Heavens* do rarely look with a malign *Aspect* upon Industry ; nor is it often seen that God doth interpose his Power to thwart an *honest Diligence*, even in common and Worldly Designs ; or if He doth, He seldom confounds it : How much more then may we be confident of his favour in those Heavenly Enterprizes, which himself hath commanded and promised his Assistance to the undertakers. And since that the most *glorious Designs* do often prove abortive for want of *Resolution*, a repulse or two ought not to *blunt*, but whet our *Desires*, *fires.* Remembring that Difficulties are the common pretences and *Mormo's* of inglorious Sloath, but fpurs and encouragements to a refolved Diligence. Nor ought any to be difcouraged from *letting down their Nets,* becaufe fome perchance have already *toiled to no purpofe:* fince by the Divine Benediction, attending our patience and perfeverance, 'tis poffible we may yet obtain fuch a lucky Draught, as that our Nets being ready to break through the multitude of Fifhes, we may be forced to *becken* to our *Friends and Partners* on the *Britifh* Shore, to come in to our affiftance. St. *Bede l. Hift. Eccl. Angl.* relates, that in the Infancy of our *Church,* fuch a difappointment happened in an unconverted part of our *Nation*; at which yet, he tells us that others, nothing difcouraged, in a fecond attempt perfected what the former had left for defperate. Even fo we overlooking all Difficulties, and *preffing* ftill *forward to the Mark, if we faint not,* may obtain that that *Prize* for which we fet forth, and accomplifh a Work greatly tending to the *Glory of God,* and to the happinefs of thefe poor Peoples Souls, no lefs than of our own. But, *O were our Duty,* (as St. *Chryf.* fweetly exhorteth, *l. 6. de Sacerd. c. 40.) of Piety and a virtuous Life faithfully complied with, we might foon, and even without Miracles, convert the World!* Wherefore, *Lift up the Hands that hang down, and the feeble Knees,* as faith the *Apoftle.* Let us be *inftant in feafon and out of feafon,* and *keep back nothing of the whole Councel of God,* that is neceffary for the Souls of Men. That fo when our Lord fhall come to require his Sheep, calling unto us, as *Auguftus* is faid to have done to *Varus,* to reftore the Souls committed to our Charge; *We may give our Account with Joy and not with Grief.* And that we now *feeding the Flock of God, and taking the overfight thereof (not by conftraint but willingly; not for filthy Lucre, but of a ready Mind)* may, *when the chief*

Shepherd

Shepherd shall *appear, receive a* Crown *of* Glory, *which fadeth not away.*

2. And for the People, I shall propose unto them three *general Rules* in this Affair to be guided by. Whereof the first is, To make the *Negro's* cafe our own, as being the beft way, to judg what is fit for others. And then to remember how unjuft it would feem to one of us, that our *different White* should deprive us of the leaft Advantage; much more of the greateft, which *Religion* is. That *Injunction* of our Bleffed Lord, *of dealing fo with all Men,* as we should upon the like change of our Fortunes expect from them, being a Principle highly Moral, and Natural; and fufficient to make us wave thofe proud diftinctions, which only avarice, and a too worthy conceit of our felves, have taught us.

3. And to this I shall, under the fame Head, add fome few other Confiderations of the fame kind, which may greatly add to our Security. As, 1. To reflect how dangerous *Extremities* are, and that as *nothing violent is lafting,* fo nothing is more *permanent* than *Moderation.* 2. To think how inconvenient this Diftance and Difference between Man and Man, *Indians* and *Negro's, English* and both, may in time prove. The *Poets* advice,

Tros Tyriûfq; mihi nullo difcrimine agetur.

being much more conducive to our Happinefs and Security. 3. To meditate what fit *Inftruments* for any State *Revolution,* fuch miferable People are; who being very *numerous,* should not be too much *Exafperated,* nor driven into *Defperation.* 4. To reflect what a reproach and difhonour to the *English Nation,* and *Government,* our *unchriftian* treating of thefe People is. 5. Wifely to look rather to the *moft lafting,* then to the *prefent Gain;* And in confequence thereof,

Not

Not to labour (so much) *for the Meat that perisheth,* &c. St. *John* 6. Lastly, To remember *at whose Hands their Blood will be required,* if they perish ; and not think with *Cain* to shift the Guilt off, by demanding, *Am I my Slaves keeper,* which certainly each of you are. And therefore to be merciful to your *own Souls,* if not to your *Slaves. He that taketh warning shall deliver his Soul,* Ezek. 33. *But otherwise his Blood shall be upon his own Head.*

4. Secondly, I shall beseech you to look unto the *Generation of God's Children* ; and to see what is done by others, whether at Home or Abroad, by our own *Countrymen,* or by *Strangers,* both in *Europe,* and in their remoter *Colonies,* and from thence to collect and imitate the best Examples. As for our own *Nation,* if we look into *New-England,* they scruple not to admit either *Negro's* or *Indians,* when capacitated and fit for it, to their very *Sacraments,* which very many of the *English* cannot obtain. The Infants also of such are allowed *Baptism*: And of the *Bermudians* I have (*Page* 143) before spoken.

5. Again, If we appeal to our Mother-Country, the respect there to them is *notorious,* and even become the Scoff of this place. 'Tis true, their *Zeal* is said of late to be much abated. But this, as 'tis the Crime of some few, whose great *Wisdom* consisteth only in *getting of Money* (the *grand Antichrist* of our *English Nation,* which, in the very letter of the Text, they exalt, ἐπὶ πάντα λεγόμενον τ̄ Θεόν, ἢ σέβασμα, *above God and Religion*:) So I doubt not but their *Impiety* will in time be better lookt into, and a stop be put to its further growth, at least there : And those *Mammonists* be obliged to a more Christian deportment and compliance with the universal practice of all Believers, especially of our *English Nation,* till now.

6. And as to *Foraign Nations* 'tis certain, that they

M   treat

treat their *Negro's* and others, both *here* and in *Europe*, as Men capacitated *for the like hopes* with themselves. And in consequence of that belief, do not only permit, but compel them to partake with themselves in *Religion.* Of whom some are daily promoted to the *Priesthood,* and other Offices in the *Church.* And I have here seen and discoursed with divers, who were brought from those parts ; which, besides some Reports of that nature which I had otherwise met with, hath ascertained me of the truth thereof. Now all these, were they not better principled, might urge the like Objections against their being made *Christians,* which our selves do here. But they are not yet arrived to that *wisdom* and fore-sight as to apprehend the *Dangers and Inconveniencies* of Religion.

7. Thirdly, I shall recommend unto them, 1. A frequent view of the *Terms,* by which only they can pretend a Right to God's Temporal *Blessings. He gave them the Lands of the Heathen,* saith *David, that they might observe his Statutes, and keep his Laws.* So that *obedience to God's Laws* can only entitle Men to the *good things* that they here enjoy : Which if referred to Christianity, doth, no question, amongst other, infer this *Duty* also. 2. And then after a serious view of the *Terms,* to see how others have fared upon the forfeiture. St. *Paul* speaking of the *Jews, Rom. 9.* hath these words, *Because of unbelief they were broken off, and thou standest by Faith.* And in the *Acts,* he bespeaks the same *Jews* to have *thrust from them the Word of Eternal Life.* And in another place not only so, but they are also charged with *forbidding the Preaching of it to the* Gentiles, *that they might be saved :* The crying Sin of these *Colonies !* From which impudent despite done to *Religion,* he ominates their speedy destruction, and that *Wrath which should* (and not long after did) *come upon them even to their utter Extermination,* 1 Thess. 2. 16.

And

And, 3*ly.* After all, to apply this unto our selves, *If God spared not the Natural Branches, how much less will he spare thee ? Be not therefore high-minded, but fear ; for otherwise thou also shalt be broken off.* Nor is this the utmost of the danger ; but there is mentioned something further, 2 Theff. 1. *The Lord Jesus shall be revealed from Heaven with his mighty Angels, in flaming Fire, taking vengeance of them that know not God, and that obey not the Gospel of our Lord Jesus Christ ; who shall be punisht with everlasting destruction from the presence of the Lord, and from the glory of his Power ; when he shall come to be admired in his Saints, and to be glorified in all them that believe.*

8. But if none of all thefe *Considerations* will prevail, the laft thing I fhall propofe, is, That you will now at length remove that *Vizard,* and undeceive the World, who have been apt hitherto, becaufe *going by that Name,* to believe you *Christians :* Which Name with · what face Men can thus ufurp, whofe practices do prove them not fo much as *tollerable Heathens,* is in truth my great wonder and aftonifhment; and whilft they retain, *Iftam in figurâ hominis feritatem & immanitatem belluæ ;* Such a brutifh *ferity* under humane appearance. Since the *Orator* (as before P. 87, 88.) informs us, *That it is more against Nature, for one Man to wrong another, for his private Gain, than Death, Poverty, Pain, or any other Calamity. That they who do hold the contrary, do feparate Man from himfelf. That he is miftaken that thinks any difcommodity either of Body or Eftate, to be forer than the Vices of the Mind. That no Man's Life can be more profitable, than fuch a difpofition of mind, not to violate any, even the moft defpicable Wretch, for his Profits fake.* Which being true, where will your pretended *Christianity* be found, who againft all Confcience and Reafon, are fo unjuft and cruel to your Slaves ? Wherefore till you can afford to

com-

comport your selves more agreeable thereto, be but so just to your selves and us, as to decline the *Name :* That so your *Inhumanity*, *Avarice*, and *Irreligion*, may no longer be a Stain and Reproach to that *Profession*; unto which otherwise the Generality will be apt to ascribe them. Nor let any one think strange of this Proposal, which is but Just and Reasonable : It being a most undoubted *Truth*, and for which, I think, I should not be afraid to become a Martyr, *That they who do industriously oppose the propagation of Christianity, especially in their own Families, can be themselves* (at most) *but Heathens*.

9. Nor let any here go about to take *Sanctuary* under that *Turkish* Tenet, *That God accepts not the Services of Slaves*. This, like the rest, being but a *poor shift*, and will hardly stand them in stead, when the *rust of their ill-gotten Treasure*, for *which they have sinned against their own Souls*, *shall be a witness against them*; it being certain, that whatever is perfect in its kind, is equally grateful to an impartial Goodness. And should any *Act* of theirs prove less perfect, yet where out of their power to remedy, it cannot be less *accepted* by Him, who requires no more than he gives, and judges by the intent, and respects *not how great*, but *how good* our Offerings are; and hath moreover by his Apostle, 2 *Cor.* 8. declared, *That if there be first a willing Mind, it is accepted according to what a Man hath, not according to what he hath not.* No act of the Soul being to be reputed faulty, for the infirmities of the Body, any more than a *Prisoner* can be accountable for his *Keepers* cruelty, or a *Slave* for his *Masters*.

10. Let not then the *Negro* too much despond, or sink under these Discouragements; but rather assure himself, That since *God cannot but have a desire to the work of his Hands*, nothing but his own neglect can prevent his Happiness: And that since He sent *his Son* to

Re-

Redeem all, there is Mercy in ſtore for him alſo. For (to apply the words of the *Evangelical Prophet* to this caſe) *the Son of the Stranger, that hath joyned himſelf to the* Lord, *is not to ſpeak, ſaying, The* Lord *hath utterly ſeparated me from his People*; *neither let the* Eunuch *ſay,* I am a dead Tree. *For thus ſaith the* Lord, *even unto them that chuſe the things that pleaſe me, and that take hold of my* Covenant, *will I give in mine Houſe, and within my Walls, a Place and a* Name, *better than of* Sons *and* Daughters, *and I will give them an everlaſting* Name, *that ſhall not be cut off.* Alſo the Sons of the Stranger *that joyn themſelves to the* Lord *to ſerve him, and to love the* Name *of the* Lord, *and to be his* Servants; *even them will I bring to my holy Mountain, and make them joyful* in my Houſe of Prayer: *Their* Burnt-offerings *and their* Sacrifices *ſhall be accepted upon mine* Altar; *for mine Houſe ſhall be called an Houſe of Prayer for all People,* Iſa. 56. Now theſe *Evangelical* Promiſes of Admittance and Acceptance being ſo general, and without any reſpect of Perſons, it cannot be doubted but theſe are comprehended in them. Wherefore, to determine all in the words of the *Apoſtle,* Gal. 3. 26, 28, 29. & 4. 7. *If thou,* O black Æthiopian, art become *Chriſt*'s Diſciple and Servant, and doſt *by Faith* truly embrace and lay hold of him, *then art thou,* as to thy Soul, and all the ends and purpoſes of the Goſpel, *no longer a Slave but a Son, and even* Abraham's Seed: *And if a Son, then an Heir of God through Chriſt according to the Promiſe: For we are all the Children of God by Faith in Chriſt Jeſus.* Unto which, neither Condition, Country, Complexion nor Deſcent, can be any Impediment. *There being in him neither* Jew *nor* Greek, Bond *nor* Free, Male *nor* Female: *For we are all one in Chriſt Jeſus.*

11. I ſhall cloſe up my Diſcourſe with that advice of *Jeremiah,* Chap. 13. 16. *Give Glory to the* Lord *your God*

M 3

before

before he cause Darkness, and before your Feet stumble upon the dark Mountains, and while ye look for Light, he turn it into the shadow of Death and make it gross Darkness : Adding only that Religious Expostulation of the *Philistine Priests and Sages,* (1 Sam. 6.) to their Princes and *Optimates,* touching the dimission of the Captivated Ark : *Wherefore do ye harden your Hearts, as the* Egyptians *and* Pharaoh *hardened their Hearts ? When he had wrought wonderfully among them, did they not let the People go and they departed ?* That is, they found it requisite and necessary to do them that Right and Justice : And it will be our Wisdom to do so too.

12. And thus have I finished this Discourse, wherein as I have not forborn to take notice of the least *Objections,* so neither, I think, have I inserted any thing that may, especially to those who understand the temper of this place, seem in the least superfluous. So that nothing being hereby left unanswered, nor any colour or *shadow of Argument* remaining, The *Question* must, I presume, be placed *beyond dispute*; nor can there be any pretence or cloak left for the Impieties here condemned. And unless the Opposers will defie the clearest *Truth,* they cannot but confess the Obligation upon their Souls for complying with this Duty, herein urged and asserted. Of which yet what may be the Issue, I shall not enquire, but rest satisfied that *I have done what I could,* and *delivered my Soul*; which I must declare that otherwise I could not. And no less shall comfort my self, that whatever shall be the success, either through any *neglect* at Home, or *opposition* here; and that, tho it should happen, which I trust it cannot, (*Truth being most powerful and must prevail,*) that *I should labour in vain,* and *spend my strength for nought and in vain,* yet surely my judgment is with the Lord, and my work with my God. Amen.

—*Nunquam successu crescat honestum,* Luc. l. 9.

The

The State of Religion in Virginia, *as it was some time before the late Rebellion, repreſented in a Letter to Sir* W. B. *then Governour thereof.*

THat I have made bold to preſent unto your *Excellency* this * mean Diſcourſe (expoſed to public view more of *Neceſſity,* and to vindicate my ſelf, than of *choice*) is

* *Then intended to be made public, but for other reaſons here omitted.*

becauſe it may no leſs need your *Patronage,* than the *Author* himſelf did, during his abode in that your *Province* of *Virginia.* A *Colony* that may be ſaid wholly to owe it ſelf to your *Excellency,* made happy by your Prudent Government, as being the Prime, if not the only *Raiſer* of her to her preſent Greatneſs; having firſt reſcued her from moſt imminent and apparent Deſtruction; whilſt by your noble and wiſe Conduct, you not only broke the force of the *Common Enemy,* but ſo utterly ſubdued, as to extinguiſh in them all hopes, and to deſtroy the very Seeds of any future Diſturbance, which might ariſe through their Occaſion.

And having like a tender *Father* nouriſhed and preſerved that *Colony* in her *Infancy* and *Non-age,* you carefully guarded her ever ſince, having ſcarce ſet Foot off that Soil for well near theſe forty Years. Under whoſe *Tutelage* ſhe is now almoſt grown Adult, needing no aſſiſtance from, but rather able to afford ſome to her Mo-

M 4

there

ther Country. So that we may without *Assentation* affirm, that your Excellency hath been no less a Sanctuary to *Virginia* in her distress, than *Virginia* hath been unto others. Which tho she hath happily since outgrown, yet your *Excellency* doth not cease still to make evident proof of your Innate Affection to her, yearly expending your proper Income and Revenue for the good of her; paying her much more Credit and Support than you receive; thereby demonstrating that the only reward you desire and wish, is that she may thrive and prosper.

But as our *Blessed Saviour* once said to the young Man in the *Gospel, Yet lackest thou one thing to be perfect;* so may we, and I fear too truly, say of *Virginia*, that there is one thing, the Propagation and Establishing of *Religion* in her, wanting; which if by your *Excellencies Piety* added, would make your *Name* great, and your *Memory* glorious; no less than that place, which hath so long been the Seat of your Government, *Happy*. For there is no pious Eye nor Heart can consider the great (Neglect shall I say? or rather) contempt of *Religion* there, without *resolving* it self *into Sighs and Tears.* It is most certain that there are many *Families*, who have never been present at any public Exercise of *Religion* since their *Importation* into that *Colony*. The *Ministers* also are most miserably handled by their *Plebeian Junto's*, the *Vesteries*; To whom the *Hiring* (that is the usual word there) and Admission of *Ministers* is solely left. And there being no Law obliging them to any more than to procure a *Lay-Reader* (to be obtained at a very moderate rate): They either resolve to have *none at all*, or reduce them to their own *Terms*; that is, to *use them how they please*, pay them *what they list*, and to *discard* them *whensoever they have a mind to it.* And this is the recompence of their leaving their hopes in *England* (far more considerable to the meanest Curate,

than

than whatever can poffibly be apprehended there)
together with their *Friends* and *Relations*, and their
Native Soil, to venture their Lives into thofe parts a-
mongft Strangers and Enemies to their Profeffion, who
look upon them as a Burden ; as being with their *Families* (where they have any) to be fupported out of
their Labour. So that I dare boldly aver, that our
Difcouragements there are much greater, than ever
they were here in *England*, under the *Ufurpers*. I
fhall, to avoid tedioufnefs and multiplicity of Examples, Inftance only in their being *hired from Year to Year*,
and made to accept of Parifhes at under Rates, which
I think was never practifed in thofe Times, efpecially
upon fuch as were approved by *their own Laws* and conformable to *their Government*, which thofe *Minifters* now
in *Virginia* in all things are to the *Government* there.

Sir, I would not be thought to fpeak this out of
any defign to difparage the Place ; It being a Country
fo *Fruitful*, and withal fo *Pleafant*, efpecially towards
the Southern parts, as *Carolina*, &c. that I do prefer it before *England* in many things ; but may juftly
equal it thereto in all ; Thofe only excepted, which
Time and multitudes of People muft produce. Only
I cannot but think it great pity, that a *Region* fo richly
furnifhed with *Bleffings of the Left*, fhould fo much
want thofe more neceffary ones *of the Right-Hand*.

Much lefs would I herein be thought to reflect upon your *Excellency*, who have always profeffed a great
tendernefs for *Church-Men*. For alas, thefe things are
kept from your Ears ; nor dare the Minifters, had they
opportunity, acquaint you with them, for fear of being
ufed worfe. And there being no *Superiour* Clergyman,
neither in *Council* nor in any place of Authority, for
them to addrefs their Complaints to, and by his means
have their Grievances brought to your *Excellencie's*
know-

knowledg, they are left without Remedy. Befides, their *Adverfaries* have that ufual craft of underhand blafting their Fame, and charging them with *Litigi-oufnefs*, (which is nothing elfe but *a fuing for their own*,) or prepoffeffing your *Excellency* with forged Stories, either by themfelves Invented, or known to be as Falfe, as the beft Evidence can make them. But yet when thereby a *fecret Prejudice* is conceived againft them, and the caufe unknown, they find it impoffible to redeem their Reputations with your *Ex-cellency*. But,

Dat veniam Corvis, vexat cenfura Columbas :

For where any thing is truly Chargeable, as is frequent amongft their *leaden Lay-Priefts* of the *Vefteries ordination* (* which make up near two thirds of the Preachers), and is both the fhame and grief of the rightly Ordained Clergie there ; Nothing of this ever reaches your *Excellencie's* Ear : Thofe hungry *Patrons* knowing better how to make benefit by *their Vices*, than by the *Vertues* of the other.

How true this is, may be gathered from the Story of a certain Writing-Mafter who came into Virginia, firft as Bifhop thereof; but that not taking, he profeffed himfelf Doctor of Divinity, and wore a Scarlet Hood in the Pulpit, going by the name of Dr. Dacres, and fhewing Orders under that Name. But, being difcovered, hath fince changed that Name to Acworth; yet to this hour continues his Preaching and Doctorfhip, if alive, which lately he was.

The Laws alfo which are tranfmitted hither to invite the Subjects into thofe Parts, are many of them fo intricate and obfcure, (not to fay contradictory and fallacious) that they feem rather to be *Traps and Pit-fals*, than Laws: I fhall inftance in two. The firft is, That wherein Servitude for four Years is made the
penalty

enalty of accepting of anothers Kindnefs (if I may
o term it) ; that is, for permitting ones felf to be
Tranfported *gratis*, when with much feeming Cur-
efie and Importunity offered unto them: For thereby
he Party (whether Minifter or other, without ex-
ception) doth, by virtue of that Law, put himfelf
nto the Tranfporters power, and is made to become
iis Servant, or to Ranfome himfelf from that Thral-
Jom and Mifery at a very great rate, perhaps four or
five times fo much as their Paffage fhould have coft
them.   A deceit which no *Englifhman*, not verfed in
thofe *American Arts* and *Frauds*, can provide againft;
and is indeed the great ftay and fupport of the *Kid-
nappers* Trade and Myftery. A Trade that, 'tis thought,
carries off and confumes not fo little as ten thoufand
People out of this Kingdom yearly ; which might have
been a defence to their Mother-Country, but now are
many of them miferably deftroyed, without any advantage to it.

The fecond is that Act, wherein, (contradictory
to it felf, no lefs than to our Act of *Uniformity*, and
to another of their own), it is declared, *That to the
intent that Servants Marriages may not be made in fecret,
they are forbidden to be publifhed* (before-hand by *Banns*,
the ufual and only way of preventing that Secrefie ,
and that under no lefs penalty than 10000 pounds
of *Tabacco* ; a Sum almoft (if not quite) double to
divers *Minifters* Incom and Allowance. And this for
a thing unto which they are bound under as great Penalties by the faid *Act* of *Uniformity*, and other Laws
enjoyning the faid Publications. Which being once
by moft of the *Minifters* of that *Colony*, in an humble
Addrefs and Petition to your *Excellency* reprefented, as
both unreafonable and unpoffible to be complied
with, (at the fame time giving in their reafons for
that

that *Allegation*); they were so far from finding Redress from the *Assembly* then sitting, unto whom it was referred, that the *Ministers* found their condition much more uneasie afterward, than it was before. Besides the present Punishing of the Promoters thereof, tho not under that, but another Guise. I might here also insert the danger which doth usually ensue to the *Minister* upon his demanding the benefit of those Laws which concern their Maintenance: This being a Crime, which no *Grandee* of any *Vestry*, throughout the Country, shall ever forgive.

To this may be added the profound Silence as to things given to Pious Uses; the not only permitting but commissioning *Lay-Men* to preach, and to enjoy four or five Parishes (but at under Rates): *Deacons* to undermine and thrust out *Presbyters*, to Administer the Sacraments, reade the Absolution, and enjoy Pluralities. Their suffering Parishes to extend to sixty or seventy Miles in length, or letting them lie void for many Years together to save Charges, (as the Metropolis, your Honour's Parish, did (as 'tis said) for near twenty Years, some little Intervals only excepted): And in a word, the permitting of all things that concern the *Church* and *Religion*, to the Mercy of the People.

One thing I had almost forgotten, and that is, besides the establishing of *Religion* amongst the *English*, the *propagating* of it amongst the *Heathen*, both *Natives* and *Slaves* also brought from other parts. Which tho, as must be piously supposed, it were the only end of God's discovering those Countries to us, yet is there lookt upon, by our new Race of *Christians*, as so idle and Ridiculous, so utterly needless and unnecessary, that no Man can forfeit his Judgment more, than by any proposal looking or tending that way.

I

I presume I need not acquaint your Excellencie how useful *Religion*, where it hath not lost its Force, (and there it ought by all means to be revived) is to the ease and support of *Government*, and may prove, to the securing of the *King*'s Interest in those *Plantations*. Nor what an excellent *Heathen* Writer tells us, *That Religion is the Cement of all Communities, and the chief Basis of Legislative Power: That it is much more easie to build a* Castle (we may also add, To plant a Colony) *in the open Air, without any ground to found it upon, than to establish a Government without* Religion. Much less that the despising of the *Ephod*, was the Rot of *Sauls* Kingdom and Government: And that the cause why *Jeroboam* is made to carry that infamous Train and Brand, Jeroboam *the Son of* Nebat, *who made Israel to sin*, nineteen times after him in sacred Scripture, was only for the contempt of *Religion*, and his committing the sacred Oracles to unclean and unholy Hands. Your *Excellency* knows all these things already, and needs no information; who doubtless are possessed with a deep inward veneration and sense of *Religion* upon a much higher *Account*, and that is *the salvation of Souls.*

However, let me be bold to be your Remembrancer, and to mind your *Excellency* how needful it is, that those good Laws which are made for the suppression of *Vice*, and for *reducing* the People from this affected *Gentilism*, to a more diligent and conscientious discharge of their Duty to *God*, (the *only sure means to retain them in their due Allegiance to their Soveraign)* be by the Inferiour Magistrates more duly executed; The *Ministers* encouraged, and all Invaders of that sacred Calling, cashired and punished for their bold and prophane *Usurpations.*

But I begin to exceed my Limits, in thus presuming
ming

ming to prescribe unto your *Excellency*, who are wise enough to effect whatsoever is necessary as to this most *Important Affair*, so soon as you shall find it expedient so to do. Wherefore beseeching your *Excellency* to excuse this Presumption, and to accept these my *weak* Performances, which I humbly submit unto your Censure, I am

Your Excellencies

Servant, and Orator,

M. G.

Psal. 119. 12. *It is time for the Lord to Work, for they have made void thy Law.*

Ezek. 8. 12. *For they say, The Lord seeth us not, the Lord hath forsaken the Earth.*

FINIS.

A
SUPPLEMENT
TO THE
Negro's & Indian's
ADVOCATE
OR,

Some further CONSIDERATIONS and PROPOSALS for the effectual and speedy carrying on of the *Negro's* Christianity in our *Plantations* (Notwithstanding the late pretended IMPOSSIBILITIES) without any prejudice to their Owners.

By *M. G.* A Presbyter of the Church of ENGLAND.

St. Luke 18. 4. *He would not for a while, but, &c.*
St. Mat. 21. 24. *Afterward he repented, and went.*

Who made you Ministers of the Gospel to the *White* People only, and not to the **Tawneys** and **Blacks** also? *Quakers* Speech to the Ministers of *Barbadoes, p.* 4. of *Negro's* Advocate.

But above all that accursed Tyranny used towards the *Souls* of those miserable Wretches, *can never sufficiently be bewailed*, who are daily assaulted by those professed Enemies of Christ, to turn *Apostates* to the *Christian* Faith, and to deny that *only Name given under Heaven*, by which they can be saved : Whereby they lye under a continual Temptation to abandon their *Religion*, that they may obtain their Liberty. *Breef for the Captives in* Algiers.

The Office for the Baptism of such as are of riper Years, may be always useful for the Baptizing of *Natives in our Plantations*, and others converted to the Faith. *Pref. to Com. Pr.*

Do in God's Name earnestly require that due and true Execution hereof be had, — *As they will answer before God for such Evils and Plagues*, wherewith Almighty God may justly punish his People for neglecting this, *&c. Act of Unif.* 1. *Eliz.*

Act. 26. 16. I have appeared unto thee for this purpose, to ordain thee a Minister, and a Witness, both of these things, which thou hast seen, and of those things, in the which I will appear unto thee.

17. Delivering thee from the People, and from the Gentiles, unto whom now I send thee,

18. To open their Eyes, and to turn them from Darkness to Light, and from the power of Satan unto God, that they may receive forgiveness of Sins, and Inheritance among them which are sanctified by Faith which is in me.

The PREFACE.

THE *Agents and Factors for the* Plantations, *being lately requir'd to give in their Reasons, for their refusing to make their* Negro's Christians, (*as if any Reasons against* Christianity *could be admitted!*) *they, it it seems, proved so masculine and strong, that the Design was instantly given up for impossible. Of these Reasons, such as they are,* * *I have here given a Specimen ; and in Answer thereto,* (*that the World may judge of their Impossibility, and withal, see how easily our People are to be satisfied in a business (even) of this Weight and Moment ;) have opposed against them only these three Proposals, as sufficient to compleat the whole Work if duly followed :* First, *That our* Planters Interest *in their* Negro's *and other Slaves, be secured.* Secondly, *That the* Ministers *there, be both obliged and encouraged (the only thing wanting) to preach to their People, touching this Duty.* Thirdly, *That their* Negro's *Sunday-Labour and Polygamie be prohibited. By the* First *of these, Their common pretence of Interest will be removed ; and all Colour for complaining upon that account, would be washt off:* Now *why this should be opposed or denied, I see not. For what Inconvenience or Prejudice can ensue to the Owner (or to us) by haveing his Right secured? And his* dearest Mammon *being safe, his Thoughts will be more at ease, and he may then be at leasure to attend upon the Duties of Religion, and to serve* Christ. *Or how, in the* Second *place, can the Ministers preaching hurt him, since at the end of the Sermon he will be left to his former Liberty ; nothing of Force or of Compulsion being in the least required, or intended ? Only* twill *be prest upon his* Conscience, *and the necessity of it will be laid before him ; but whether he will hear, or whether he will forbear, will remain as much at his own choice, as it did before. Tho it may not be doubted, but that whilst some of the looser sort shall, with the* Athenian *Atheists and* Epicures Act. 17. *only mock and make sport, (or, which is worse, Obstruct our Endeavours ;) others, like the devout* Areopagite, *will be affected with the heavenly Doctrine, and perswaded to cleave unto it, and to obey the* Truth ; *And then our Labour will not be wholly lost. But rather from these small beginnings, a great Door and effectual will be opened unto us, notwithstanding the many* Adversaries : *And this little Leaven may in time grow sufficient to season, not only the lesser Islands, but also the vaster* Continent *of our* America. *It being* Im-

* Being no other then what I had before taken notice of *Page* 101, 102, 104, 109, 139. &c of the Negro's Advocate.

possible

possible that Christianity should be without Followers, if allowed but Scope and Liberty, and a free Course, tho other Means and Encouragements should be wanting. And for the Third, The profit from thence arising, is so sordid and inconsiderable and withal so utterly inconsistent with Christianity (especially *ours) that, no considerate or discreet Person who owns this, can do less than abhor (pardon the Expression, I hope, it will not be offensive in this Case) and be ashamed of that. Thus these insuperable Difficulties are, we see, in a Moment put to flight, and a most smooth and easy Path is chalked out to this Work, notwithstanding the Impossibilities. So that nothing besides a supine Sloath on the one hand, or direct Irreligion on the other, can cause any further Stop to our Negro's Christianity; and we shall be for ever left without Excuse, should it be any longer neglected, or opposed. And God may justly take it out of our hands, and transfer it to others, who will do it. And then those Myriads of People, who, if by us initiated into Christianity, might (so far) have been a Strength and Defence to our Religion (in this time of its distress,) being first Instructed in a way so opposite thereto, will afford the same Advantage against it. So that to neglect or hinder this Work, is a manifest betraying of the Protestant Interest, and no less an advancing of Popery: which they that do, can be no other than open Enemies to the King and Kingdom. Nor in the last place, can the Ministers be displeased hereat, but rather be invited to give God thanks for the opportunity. For, if this be not needful, neither is their other Preaching; and all the World may as well be saved without Christianity, as those Negro's. But if without becoming *Christians, they cannot be saved, then are we by this unfaithful Silence, as much as in us lyeth, the cause of their Damnation. And here let no one think strange of my earnestness herein, which I conceive to be my Duty both as a Clergy-man and a Christian : being also loath to be baffled (by such Paultry Objections) in so good and righteous a Cause; To promote which, as it was the sole End of my returning home from those parts, so. I am fully purposed (by God's assistance) not to desist from the pursuit (non si capiundos mihi sciam esse inimicos omnes [Colonos]), notwithstanding any the greatest discouragements whatsoever, until arrived within a prospect of its accomplishment.

Marginal notes:
" Who have so high a Veneration for the Sunday, even beyond all other Christians.

* See Acts 4. ver. 12. As also the late Alg. Breef, That only Name, &c.

Salus hominis opus dignum Deo. *Tert.*

A SUPPLEMENT to the Negro's and Indian's, ADVOCATE,

OR,

Some further PROPOSALS, &c.

§ I.

BEfore we enter upon this Debate, to prevent all troublesome Clamors and Objections against it, upon the score of *Interest*, this Position should first be laid down, and as a Principle fixt and Eternal, and from which a true Christian cannot recede, be resolved on, (*viz.*) That no Interest how great or (otherwise) just soever, may be admitted to stand in Competition with *Christianity*. The Question (else) being the same, as between *Christ* and *Barabbas*, that is, whether of the two, *Religion* and the *Glory of God*, with the *good of Souls*; or worldly *Pelf* and filthy *Lucre* shall be preferred. And then this Position being first laid down, afterwards to fall to considering of the best Expedients for the carrying of it on, with the least prejudice to that *Interest*; if any such would happen to interpose. And this would be to act like *Christians*; and might (besides) in the end prove as little hurtful to any just Interest, as that other Method so much in fashion, of consulting *Interest* first, and then leaving *Christianity* to be contented with such favours and kindnesses, as the *Devil* and *Mammon* shall at last please to afford her. *Were this done, they'd quickly find out expedients to save their Interest.*

And here also in this Consideration, we are especially to avoid Splitting upon this Solecism, both in Policy and Discretion, and against which, *Ecclus* hath so wisely cautioned us, ch. 37. *v.* 11. [*Not to ask Counsel for Religion of one that hath no Religion, nor of Justice of him that hath no Justice*] *nor of a Coward about Matters of War, nor of a Merchant concerning Exchange, nor of a Buyer concerning selling* &c. *for such will counsel for themselves,* ver. 8. So likewise for a *Christian* not to be guided or led by *Self-ended* Men, Enemies to his Profession, in these Debates and Proposals made for the Advancement of it. Such being only

[This Part of the verse] is not found in the present Translation, but in some other it is, particularly that of *Geneva*.

only like to raife *Obstructions*, as hitherto they have always done ; and (as lately) to render that for impoffible, which has not the leaft difficulty in it, where a right Method is ufed for effecting it.

No more are we to proceed herein, by the fole Advice of Perfons *unacquainted* with the true State and Condition of the places where this Settlement or Converfion is to be wrought. Such, tho never fo difcreet and wife as to o her matters here at home, being as it were wholly blind and in the dark, as to Affairs there. And therefore are almoft equally unlikely, even with the formen, (unlefs by accident) to give proper and fit Directions for the happy promoting and carrying on of any good Defign, whether in *Church* or *State*, for the benefit of thofe Parts.

§ II.   Thefe things being agreed on , we muft then fall to confider of the People amongft whom we are to take our lot, and thereto to have an efpecial regard : As, whether they be *Slaves*, fubject to the *Englifh*, fuch as moft of the *Negro's* there are ; or *free People* living of themfelves, either amongft, or diftant from, the *Englifh* ; fuch as moft of the *Indians* on the Continent (in *Virginia*, &c.) are. Or laftly, whether this is to be performed by way of further Setling and Eftablifhment, even amongft the *Englifh* themfelves, which alfo is no lefs neceffary.   In all which Cafes, we are to act only by *prudential Rules*, and to proceed therein by *different Methods* and Wayes : That, 'tis poffible, being lefs fit or convenient for the one, which is only proper and neceffary for the other ; and fo alfo on the contrary. Nor in any of thefe is any thing of Force, or of Compulfion to be ufed : but all muft be carried on quietly and by degrees, as God fhall pleafe to favour our Endeavours with fuitable and profperous Opportunities.

§ III.   Now concerning the *Negro's*, whom I fhould think fit to be firft taken in hand (as being the eafieft Task, would their * Owners be perfwaded to confent thereto; & the moft abfolutely neceffary, this neglect being the moft fcandalous, and withal, the moft impoffible to be defended or excufed :)   The firft and great ftep will be to procure (what I but juft mentioned) their *Owners confent*, as being to be fuppofed *averfe* thereto : not altogether, as is here believed, out of *Intereft* (it being already fecured to them by Laws of their own;) but by reafon of the trouble, and the fancied *needlefsnefs* of the Work ; and

* How much fuller of Generofity and Zeal for their Religion, the *Algier Pirates* are (fee the *Breef*) than thefe *nominal Chriftians*? For thofe do invite their *Slaves* and *Captives* with the affurance of *Libertie*, to embrace their *Superftition*: while thefe to avoid that danger, do induftioufly conceal their *Religion* rom them.

and to prevent all danger from their Slaves being furnisht with knowledge, consequent, they conceive, thereto. However, because they pretend the other (and something there may be in that too,) to take off that *pretence*, it will be requisite,

1. That a * Law be enacted to confirm such Laws of theirs, as are or shall be hereafter made to *secure their just Interest* in their Slaves ; That they may thereby be continued in their present State of *Servitude*, notwithstanding their being afterward *baptised*.

2. That all *unjust* Interests, and *ungodly* Advantages arising from their Slaves *Sunday-labour* and *Polygamie* (neither of them sufferable among *Christians*) be upon severest Penalties prohibited ; and this as well to the *unbaptised*, as to the rest.

* Such a Law could not, as has been feared, be any *Prece-dent* for *slavery*, where it has before been always practised : and they having already made Laws among themselves for the same purpose. *Till such a Law may be obtained, the *Bermudian* Caution of *Indentures* for ninty-nine Years Service might be used, that is, if they think their own Laws not sufficient.

Nor will this (but much less the other) be *grievous* to the Slave, as is *pretended*; There being some of them that live *single*; Others that content themselves only with *one Wife* ; And the rest taking the Libertie of *more*, only out of a *Licentious* and rambling *humor*, and by their *Master's Connivance* and Toleration ; Who esteeming them but as *Cattle*, and desirous of their *Encrease*, are apter to encourage, than to restrain them from it. But having such an *absolute* Authority and Command over them, might with a bare check, or but a frown, break them of it. And this may be inferred from the *Virginia Negro's*; who, tho imported from the same places, are not (so far as I could learn) addicted to *Polygamie* ; but rather of themselves choosing to follow the Custom of the *English*, to whom they are Slaves there.

These *pretences* being thus fairly removed, if any *Aversion* still remains, (as 'tis to be feared there will, and that for the truest Reasons, * above mentioned,) they must afterwards be invited thereto by good *Sermons* & *Books*, Preacht and Writ upon this Subject, and by discoursing with them in *private*. As also by the Example of the *Ministers* themselves in their *Families*. And lastly, (and which will do more then all the rest) by *Encouragments* from the *Government*. Likewise, it might be remembred, what I have heard affirmed, that there is a certain Clause, always inserted in their *Charters* and *Patents*, for * the *Propagation of*

§ IV.

* (viz.) Of the *trouble*, and of the supposed *needlesness* of this *Work*, &c.

* Whether this be so or not, I am sure, 'tis the chief reason Assigned by most of our Writers and Historians for God's goodness to us in these Discoveries.

Christianity

Christianity there; never hitherto (except by the *New-England* Men) in the least complyed with; but rather with their *utmost* care and *vigilancie* obstructed by them.

§ V.   Another way, and which 'tis possible might prove most effectual, would be to get this impiety decryed here in *England*, where our *Planters* have an extraordinary *Ambition* to be *thought well of*, and thereby to *shame* them into *better Principles*. Now this is to be done; First, by sending some *grave* and *discreet* Men, (Persons of *Esteem* and *Repute* with the more *eminent* Merchants here, who trade into those *parts*,) to perswade and convince them of the Duty and Necessity thereof, and to invite them to endeavour the *procuring* of such a *Law*, as I have before mentioned. Also by *Sermons* at *Court*; and in the *City*, *especially this ensuing Lent*; this being as much (perchance a great deal more) needing to be repented of, because as likely to *provoke* God's *Wrath*, as other sins. And lastly by the *Ministers* frequent inveighing against this *impietie*, in other of the chief *Cities* and Sea-port *Towns*, to which the *Traders* from those places do most resort. But above all a *General Fast* to implore the *divine Benediction* upon this Work, would give the World such notice, and so inflame the publick Zeal at the news of this strange *Irreligion*, that nothing can be supposed more conducive to the *destroying* of it. For hereby each *good Christians* Mouth must upon every occasion be opened against them, and so in a short time would force them to yield. And when in the *Plantations* it should come to be understood that their *impiety* was so *decryed* and *odious* here, it would go near to fall even of it self. Besides the *Quakers* (who with the *New-England Men*, are the *only* Witnesses of this Truth in those Parts; and whose Meetings the *Negro's* are therefore strictly prohibited) might be something instrumental hereto, and would be good enough to help to dispute them out of their *brutish* Gentilism.

§ VI.   Now for the *Ministers* in the Plantations, it will be requisite that they be obliged *each first Sunday* (at least) of every Moneth, to preach to their Charges upon this Subject; and earnestly to press it upon their Consciences. But more especially to be *exemplary* therein in their *own Families*; both *Catechising* and *Baptising* their Slaves, (where they have any) as soon as they shall be found fit; and that openly in the *Church*, for the Example of others.

And that no *Awe* nor *Fear* may remain upon their Spirits, it will be requisite that a sufficient Maintainance be settled upon them for life, without dependence upon the *Arbitrary* favour of *Vestries*.

The

This they would do of their own accord, were but that necessity of Christianity § 1. once resolved on.

The several Governours also should be obliged to protect them therein against abuses. But to put the sharper edge upon their Zeal, some *certainty* of Preferment should be proposed to them upon their return for *England*, after some 5 or 7 Years continuance in this service there. The want whereof (at least in the *Performance*) both will, and has been , the great occasion of this sad neglect hitherto, and the very bane of all *Religion* in those parts. It being apt to be lookt upon as want of Discretion, for Men to draw upon themselves nothing but ill usage there, to be certainly entertained with *worse* here; and as one saith, to adventure the *getting of broken Heads in the Churches service, afterwards at their return to be rewarded with that which shall break their Hearts too.* Besides, there should some regard be had of their *Degrees* in the *Universities*; as also for enlarging the *Terme* for *Lapse of livings,* (or provision for Admission by *Proxie*;) the *Terme* at present prescribed and limited by Law, being much too short and narrow to make a *Patron*'s kindness useful to a *Minister* abroad upon this *Service*. And it being but an an ill *Encouragement*, and no way becoming *Christian* Government for Men (running such *Hazards*, upon so important a **Work**), thereby to be placed under greater disadvantages, than they could, had they remained idle at home.

Now for the *Planter's* late Objections against this Work, as I have heard them represented (and I believe they are the best they had), tho I have before taken notice of them (which their being both asserted and credited here, doth very much justify) yet I shall again repeat and briefly answer them, *such as they are,* being indeed either *false,* or *frivolous,* or both : and such as will suffice to satisfie us, that they who can openly affirm and maintain such things here, may not be unapt to *believe* and *practise* worse there. But they are these;

§ VII.

Even to the *Brutality* of their *Negros.*

1. They object their *Negro*'s want of *English*; Whereas 'tis certain that there are some thousands of them, who understand *English*, no worse than our own People. *Let them begin with those.*

2. That it would make them *less governable;* the contrary to which is experimentally known amongst their Neighbours, both *French* & *Spaniards* in those parts. Now 'twould be too great a blemish to the *Reformation*, to suppose that *Popery* only makes its Converts better, but *Protestancy* worse; as this Allegation being admitted, it must be granted. And to prevent any fond conceit in them of Libertie, (an especial Branch of the same *Article*,) if there be any such danger, let two or three of each great *Family* be first baptised

As Sr *Ch. W.* late Governour of *Mevis,* & *St. Christophers,* & who has been amongst them, will testifie.

tifed; whereby the rest seeing them continued as they were, that Opinion would soon vanish: As may be concluded from the like Experiment upon another like foolish perswasion, (viz.) of their *returning into their own Country upon their Death*; confuted by fixing *Negro's* Head upon a Pole. Besides, there cannot be the least ground for this fear, unless all, whether *fit* or not, should at once be *baptifed*, which were a madness to suppose. Nor is it to be imagined that they should only be *baptifed*, the bare outward *Rite* being little available, without underftanding it; Which would take them off from harbouring such *idle* Hopes and vain *Imaginations*, if before embraced by them.

3. As for their pretended Averfion to Chriftianity, the contrary thereto is known of moft of them. And tho it is to be confeffed that fome are more carelefs and indifferent (having bin taught by the *Englifh* to be *needlefs for them*) yet for the general they are obferved to be rather *ambitious* of it. Nor, I dare affirm, can any fingle *Inftance* of fuch *averfion* in any one of them, be produced.

4. As to their (alike pretended) *Stupidity*, there is as little truth therein: divers of them being known and confeffed by their *Owners*, to be extraordinary *Ingenious*, and even to exceed many of the *Englifh*. And for the reft, they are much the fame with other People, deftitute of the means of knowledge, and wanting *Education*.

5. One thing more there remains to be added, of which, tho they may be moft afraid, yet they carefully keep it to themfelves, and that is the poffibility of their Slaves Expectation, not of *Freedom*, but of more *merciful Ufage* from them. (which is but reafon they fhould have, whether made Chriftians or not;) As, That their frequent *Emafculatings, Amputations* of *Leggs*, cropping off of Ears (and of *Heads* too), fcant Allowance for Food and *Cloaths*, and (often) no lefs *working*, than *ftarving* them to *Death*, and their unmerciful *Correction* of them, will not be fo commendably practifed upon them, when (nor now by) *Chriftians*, as they are thought fafe and allowable in their prefent State of *Brutality* and *Gentilifm*. And this is the true meaning of their fecond Objection, wherein they pretend it will make them *lefs Governable*.

See Negro's Advocate, P. 40. 41. 11 &c.

VIII. And thus I fuppofe it is evident enough, how thin and flender their *Fig-leafe* Reafons and Objections againft our *Negro's Chriftianity*, are: Yet have been thought *fufficient* hitherto, (and, may they be fuffered, are ftill like) to be made the pious *Pretences* for the *hindering* thereof; And at the fame time, for allowing a free

Courfe

Courfe to Gentilifm, and that under a *Chriftian Go-vernment* ; * together with the permiffion of in-numerable other the groffeft *Impieties.* Which rather than they fhould be any longer continued, and God be thereby difhonoured, it were pre-ferrable that the places themfelves *were all under water.* But however, in the mean time, a more accurfed *Tiranny over the Souls of thofe miferable Wretches,* (I fpeak only the Language of the late *Breef*) has thereby been exercifed, then that *never fufficiently to be bewailed,* (to the Honour of Church and Nation be it fpoken,) practifed upon their Cap-tives, by the *lefs inhumane* * *Algerines.*

* Which had it not at firft been permitted to thefe, per-haps that other had never happened.

* Who do endeavour to fave their Souls, (would their way do it) while they detain in bondage their bodies.

§ IX. Yet now after this, if *difficulties* fhall ftill be urged, (as no doubt but there will) and this Work upon that *ftale pretence* muft be further neglected and deferred ; I fhall in oppofition thereto, be bold to make fome few demands : As, what thofe *difficulties* fhould be, which are fo much greater, it feems, than thofe our *Anceftors* encountered with, even in *Pagan* Regions, and happily overcame ? Whether we ever *tryed* how *difficult* the Work was, thereby to fatisfie our felves, whether (indeed) it be fuch as it is apprehended (or, at leaft, *pretended* ?) And whether fuch a trial would not juftify us more, than thus, without trying, to conclude it *Impoffible* ? But if it be *impoffible,* why do we *pray* for it, fince all fuch *Pray-ers* muft be vain & fuperfluous, and therefore unlawful ; and why then are they not razed out of our *Liturgy?* But is it *impoffible* for us to endeavour the fecuring of our Peopl's *Intereft;* Or for the *Minifters* there, to preach to them, and to prefs the *neceffity* of this *Duty* to their People ; Which *they have before Vowed to do, fealing the fame with the bleffed Sacrament, at their Ordinations* ; Or to begin *at home,* with thofe of *their own Families* ? Or fuppofe they fhould be ftill backward, are there no ways to *ftir them up,* and to provoke their *Induftry,* as well to this, as to other (lefs neceffary) Works ; Or cannot they be minded thereof by Letters and *Precepts* (*Valeant quantum va-lere poffunt*) armed with fuitable Motives and Arguments to *excite* their Zeal, never omitted in any cafe elfe, where the defign has been thought *worth the pains* and trouble of attempting ? And why fhould the promoting of *Chriftianity* (under a *Chriftian* Government, and even in *Chriftian* Fami-lies,) be now fo much harder, than heretofore it was amongft *Heathens* & *Perfecutors* ? or for *Proteftants,* than for *Papifts* ? and for *Us,* than for the *New-England* Men ? Or, that having formerly been able to reduce the wildeft *Out-laws,* it fhould prevail nothing upon better People, pretended-ly (at leaft) its *Friends,* and (outwardly) *Proffeffors* of it ; And who (ef-pecially after fufficient means ufed for their Conviction, and the Neceffity

thereof

thereof made out to them) must have far less pretence of Reason for opposing it, than the old *Gentiles* had?

Now if these things be *Impossible*, or *Difficult*, I must then confess, that we still may, with *as little Conscience* and *Christianity* as we have done hitherto, let this Work sleep and rest till another Age, when the *Times* shall prove more *auspicious*, and the *Powers* more *favourable*, and those obstructing *Difficulties* and *Impossibilities* shall be all removed; That is, till the Evil be grown matterless, and the *Curse of God*, now in the pursuit, has overtaken us, and fully revenged the Cause of his *Name*, and of the *numberless Souls*, who already have, and are hereby still in danger to perish, through this most *unchristian* and *scandalous* Neglect; and which till it ceases, and this * accursed thing be removed, from among us, and (to use the *Philistine Sages* expression, *1 Sam. 6. 5.*) We do give Glory to the God of *Israel*, In vain shall we expect, *that he will lighten His hand from off us, and from off our Gods*; (our Princes and Rulers,) *and from off our Land.*

* See the *Coll.* for the late Fast, *Decemb. 22. 1680.* and the *Alg. Brief.*

In short, there is nothing upon Earth more *fecible* than this Design, were it but *heartily undertaken*, and, as I have said, *a right Method used for the effecting of it.* But if we shall *suffer* our selves to be baffled and frightned out of our Understandings and Reason by *bold Affirmers, Enemies* to *Pietie* and to *all Religion*, and who make *Mammon* their God, and shall quietly and contentedly sit down satisfied with their idle and false pretences, without the inquiring into the *Merit* and *Truth* of them; As it is a most infallible Sign of our *little Affection* thereto; So it is as sad an *Omen* of the less *hopes*, or even *possibility*, of its being ever effected, but by *other hands*; which it will not be *Honourable*, *Happy* nor *Safe* for us to *expect*, or *see*.

As if St. *Paul* should have asked *Elymas* the Sorcerer leave (*Act. 13.*) to preach to the *Deputie*.

Vicit uno verbo, quam cito?

And so much shall suffice for this first part, touching the promoting of *Christianity* amongst our *Negro-Slaves* in the *Plantations*: Concerning the free Tributary *Indians* and the *English* (each of them a Task of the like *difficulty* with the former), I shall hereafter *speak*; as what I *have now said* shall find *Approbation*.

Phil. 1. 28. *In nothing terrified by your Adversaries, which is to them an evident token of Perdition, but to you of Salvation.*

Magna est veritas [*Christiana*], *& prævalebit.*

FINIS.

Printed in the United States
221174BV00002B/1/A